GRAY
MATTER

The Teen Brain

GRAY
MATTER

GRAY
MATTER

The Teen Brain

Sherre Florence Phillips

Series Editor
Eric H. Chudler, Ph.D.

CHELSEA HOUSE
PUBLISHERS
An imprint of Infobase Publishing

The Teen Brain

Chelsea House
An imprint of Infobase Publishing
132 West 31st Street
New York NY 10001

Library of Congress Cataloging-in-Publication Data
Phillips, Sherre Florence.
  The teen brain / Sherre Florence Phillips.
    p. cm. — (Gray matter)
  Includes bibliographical references.
  ISBN-13: 978-0-7910-9415-0 (hardcover)
  ISBN-10: 0-7910-9415-4 (hardcover)
  1. Brain—Juvenile literature. 2. Teenagers—Juvenile literature. I. Title.
  QP376.P48 2007
  612.8'2—dc22   2007000394

Chelsea House books are available at special discounts when purchased in bulk quantities for businesses, associations, institutions, or sales promotions. Please call our Special Sales Department in New York at (212) 967-8800 or (800) 322-8755.

You can find Chelsea House on the World Wide Web at http://www.chelseahouse.com

Text and cover design by Terry Mallon

Printed in the United States of America

Bang EJB 10 9 8 7 6 5 4 3 2 1

This book is printed on acid-free paper.

All links and Web addresses were checked and verified to be correct at the time of publication. Because of the dynamic nature of the Web, some addresses and links may have changed since publication and may no longer be valid.

Contents

1 | A New Take on the Teen Brain

The teenage years. Most kids at about the age of 9 or 10 cannot wait for their thirteenth birthday, when they officially become teenagers. Yet most young adults declare that they would never want to go back. Is it any wonder? For many, the adolescent period is a blurry haze of inquiry and exploration. Self-esteem is shaky at best, buffeted by waves of emotional highs and lows. The icing on the cake is an unpredictable, uncontrollable mix of pimples, puberty, and peer pressure.

The attitude of many adults offers little comfort to adolescents. Many adults remember what went right in the teenage years and have long since suppressed unhappy memories of that period of their lives. Parents can be taken by surprise when their own child stumbles on his or her journey through adolescence and are often unsure about how to help their teen navigate the troubled waters.

The physical and emotional transformations that accompany adolescence used to be attributed solely to hormones. **Hormones** are chemicals that are released by glands into the bloodstream that can have powerful effects on the body. At the onset of puberty, large concentrations of the male and female sex hormones are released. The male sex hormone, **testosterone**, triggers the development of physical traits typical of males and the female sex hormone, **estrogen**, initiates the development of female traits. Hormones are an important trigger for some of the changes that take place during the teenage years, but they are only part of the story.

In the last few years, there has been a virtual revolution in the understanding of adolescent development. Scientists have looked beyond hormones and discovered that the brain is still under construction throughout the teenage years. In addition, different parts of the brain, each responsible for a specific behavior or a specialized aspect of information processing, are maturing on their own timetables. Some portions of a teen's brain may be able to digest information just like that of an adult, whereas other areas are still developing.

Teens have a difficult time pinpointing what happens when puberty strikes. They cannot say why they suddenly begin knocking heads with parents over issues that had not been a problem for the first 11 or 12 years of their lives. Fourteen-year-old Jesse explained it as eloquently as anyone. "It's not like I woke up one morning when I was 12 and a half and thought, 'I'm going to rebel.' It's just that I didn't think I should be treated like a kid anymore." "For me," Jasmine recalled, "it all got out of control when I started high school. I saw all the things the older kids got to do, but my parents wouldn't let me do *anything*." Then Jasmine laughed and said, "I decided that I'd do it anyway." Jeff had been sitting quietly, listening during this conversation among close high school friends. Finally he said, "I think the problem is that we are changing in big ways when we are teenagers, but our parents don't seem to change with us. That makes us crazy." After a pause, he continued, "We need to learn about the world, but our parents seem to be afraid to let us. Here I am at 15 and I still have some of the same rules as when I was 12!"

Most of the articles and books that describe the changes that are taking place in the adolescent brain are written for parents and educators. Usually the author jokes that new brain research confirms what parents had always thought, that their teen's brain goes crazy when puberty hits. Of course, that is not what happens. The truth is that adolescents seem to be as interested as anyone in what is going on in their brains once the avalanche of puberty-related changes hits. Yet authors seem to avoid talking to teens about puberty, assuming that they do not care about all the boring scientific details.

Here is an example of how much teens do care: As part of a health education program, more than 150 sixth grade students were asked to write down whatever questions they might have about puberty. During the program, the physicians and staff who conducted the study answered all the questions. Later the youths' questions were grouped into general categories to give scientists studying health education an idea about the concerns facing young adolescents. Categories included questions about growth changes, genital development, psychological changes, reproduction, timing of puberty, the opposite sex, and so on.

The questions were submitted anonymously, but the students were asked to give their gender, age, and race, and to complete a self-assessment questionnaire about their level of pubertal maturation. This gave the investigators an opportunity to find out if different age groups or genders had different types of concerns. They compiled all the information and discovered that teens of all categories are most interested in knowing the science behind puberty. A whopping 88% of the questions focused on the biological aspects of puberty. Undoubtedly, teens are intrigued about what is going on in their brains.[1]

Until only recently, little research had been done specifically on brain structure and function during the adolescent years. Scientists assumed that the brain developed in the first 3 to 5 years of life. After that, kids got smarter by packing their brains full of life experiences. However, in the last decade, scientists have learned that substantial brain growth and development accompanies puberty. Consequently, research on the adolescent brain has exploded. The goal of this book is to provide teens with a broad general description of some of the findings from this research. The focus is on the most significant brain changes between the onset of puberty and adulthood, particularly those that explain the major emotional and **cognitive** (intellectual) challenges that face adolescents.

■ **Learn more about the contents of this chapter** Search the Internet for *developmental psychology*, *neuroscience*, and *brain research*.

2 | What Is Adolescence?

Sean had just turned 14 the summer before his freshman year in high school. He had sky blue eyes that nearly always twinkled, and his lopsided grin was infectious. Sean was full of mischief. He drove the teachers crazy with his impromptu antics. The other students competed to be around Sean so that they could be in on the fun. But Sean was in agony. He had shown no signs of starting puberty—at least not the signs that matter to him, such as growing taller and getting bigger muscles. Nearly everyone was taller than him—boys and girls alike. Sean was a good athlete and had been the starting point guard on his junior high school basketball team. But the high school coaches did not seem to take him seriously. Sean figured it was because of his size and he could understand why. He was finding it difficult to hold his own physically on the court, particularly with the fully developed upperclassmen.

Sean began to grow faster during that school year. His mom regularly measured his height and made marks on the closet door to show him that he was growing. But in his opinion, he couldn't grow fast enough. All the other kids seemed to be growing too and Sean worried that he would never catch up. He continued to devote himself to basketball, working as hard as he could in practice but sitting on the bench in games. Sean clung to his role as the class clown. It was about the only way he could stand out. One of Sean's favorite comedic subjects was his own height. He frequently boasted about how he was "big man on campus"—in the grade school. Sean was hurting inside but he would never let the other kids know.

By the end of Sean's junior year, he had grown to what he described as the "majestic" height of about 5'9". He had given up his dreams of playing on the varsity basketball team. However one afternoon, after Sean had entertained everyone in the cafeteria with his pantomime of running into an invisible wall when putting his lunch tray away, the drama teacher approached Sean and suggested he try out for the spring play. The rest is history, as they say.

Sean graduated from a performing arts school in New York City. As a senior he was given one of the meatiest roles in the school's spring performance. The solo dance that he performed in one scene nearly stole the show, and Sean reveled in the attention. Sean never grew to be tall, and he still occasionally wishes he could be a little taller. But he has made peace with the cards that his genes dealt him.

Like Sean, at some point or another, most teens feel uncomfortable with their particular situation. This should come as no surprise since adolescence is a time of enormous transition. During the teenage years, a virtual metamorphosis takes place. Kids become adults. However, in the process they experience enormous biological, cognitive, and emotional transformations.

This chapter offers a cursory review of the physical and psychological transformations that accompany adolescence. Before delving into these details, let's consider what the term "adolescence" means and when it begins.

DEFINITION OF ADOLESCENCE

Adolescence is characterized as the period of biological transition between childhood and adulthood. The onset of adolescence is heralded by a significant biological marker—puberty.

Figure 2.1 Each individual physically matures at a different rate. Some generalizations can be made, however, when comparing males and females. For example, girls tend to reach their maximum height earlier than boys.

The age of onset of puberty varies among children. Each body matures in a disjointed fashion so that different traits of puberty (e.g., pimples, body hair, and sexual development) emerge in an unpredictable sequence that typically spans multiple years (Figure 2.1). Even more vague are the criteria for when adolescence ends and adulthood starts. Most would say that one is an adult when one assumes all the rights, responsibilities, and roles of an adult. In some cultures, this may be as soon as sexual maturity is achieved. These societies may still need the labor of young people, so as soon as childhood ends, adolescents are expected to marry and assume the role of an adult. In other cultures, adolescents are not considered emotionally mature enough to be adults.

In the current American culture, the age at which adult responsibilities are conferred to youth is highly variable. For those entering the military, adultlike behavior, such as maintaining high levels of performance under extreme stress, is expected at the age of 18. Yet automobile insurers seem to believe that young people are immature and reckless drivers and thus are not eligible for discounted insurance until the age of 25. In struggling to define adolescence, Dr. David Walsh, a psychologist who has spent years counseling youths and their families, described adolescence as an "in-between" stage. He stated that adolescence is "*determined not so much by what it is but by what it is not. Adolescence is not childhood, and it is not adulthood; it is the period in between those two stages.*"[2]

AGE OF ONSET OF PUBERTY

Most young people are uncomfortable with the early signs of puberty—whenever they arrive. Those who enter puberty early often receive unwanted attention from the opposite sex and may experience envy and taunting by peers of the same sex. Those who start late feel left behind by their peers and may have low self-esteem. Unfortunately there is such a huge range in ages for starting puberty that few youths feel that their experience is "normal." In fact, there is not even a typical age when most kids begin to experience symptoms of puberty. Some literature may report an average age for onset of puberty for girls and boys, but the enormous variability in the population makes a mathematical average almost meaningless.

Thus, the most common method for reporting age of onset of puberty is to give a range in ages, during which normal children enter puberty. For girls, it is "normal" to start puberty anywhere between the ages of 8 and 14. For boys, it is normal to start puberty anywhere between the ages of 10 and 15. Even these averages differ depending on the study cited. Therefore, the take-home message is that each child has his or her own internal clock for puberty, and starting puberty either slightly earlier or later than the ranges given above is probably nothing to be alarmed about. In fact, one study suggests that even if a child begins to show signs of onset of puberty extremely early, they may not progress through the subsequent stages of puberty early. For example, girls as young as 4 years of age can enter the earliest stage of breast development, but their sexual development does not progress for years. In fact, the girls were no more likely (on average) to begin menstruating early than their counterparts whose breasts began to develop at a later age.

A point that needs to be stressed is that starting puberty is only a first step in the process. Typically the first sign in both boys and girls is the appearance of dark, coarse hair under the arms and in the pubic region. Additionally, the first phase of breast development may accompany the appearance of pubic hair in girls. After the initial signs of puberty appear, other features of sexual maturation emerge gradually over time. About 3 to 4 years after onset of puberty, adolescents have completed the process of sexual maturation and are capable of creating children of their own.

BIOLOGICAL DEVELOPMENT

There are several major developmental benchmarks that are achieved during adolescence; the most well known is the physical maturation that accompanies puberty. Before puberty, both boys and girls manufacture about the same modest amounts of male and female hormones. Then at puberty, the brain signals the body to begin producing increased hormones specific to the genetic sex of the child. (Later in the book, we will consider in detail how the brain signals onset of puberty.) At puberty, boys begin to produce high levels of testosterone (the male sex hormone). In girls, estrogen and **progesterone** (the female sex hormones) levels increase. These hormones have many effects on the body.

Biological Changes in Males

The most important impact of testosterone is the growth and maturation of the primary sex organs, the testes and scrotum. Once the testes mature, they produce viable sperm and the male is capable of impregnating a female. Beginning at puberty and throughout life, males can have spontaneous erections without any sexual trigger for reasons that remain unclear. Since this can happen at any time and anywhere it can be excruciatingly embarrassing for self-conscious young teenage boys. Nocturnal emissions of semen (wet dreams) are another normal aspect of male sexual development, but they may not occur in every pubertal male.

Puberty also causes increased production of growth hormones, the trigger for the famous growth spurt of puberty. Growth speeds up spectacularly in the first half of puberty, continues for about 2 to 3 years, and slows considerably by the end of puberty. During the growth spurt, the body lengthens, and the overall shape of an individual begins to show gender-specific features. For example in males, shoulders broaden and muscle mass increases dramatically. The larger muscles are a result of testosterone, which causes individual muscle fibers to get bigger. Another effect is that each muscle fiber gets much stronger, so the pubertal male is often much stronger than females and prepubertal males.

Male patterns of hair growth appear in puberty. The first changes include dark coarse hair on the genitals and under the arms. Later, dark hair will also emerge on the face and chest. The density and distribution of body hair is largely under genetic

Table 2.1 Stages of Puberty in Boys

Age Range (Years)	Features	What Happens
11–14	Coarse body and facial hair	Hair usually begins to grow on various parts of the body. Hair can continue to spread to other parts of the body until a young man reaches about age 20.
11–15	Voice changes	Vocal cords become longer and thicker and the voice becomes lower.
13–16	External genitalia develop	Increased growth of the penis and scrotum starts and continues until adult size is reached about 2 years later. Thinning and reddening of the scrotum occurs around age 12 years. During puberty, boys tend to get erections more frequently, although spontaneous erections may occur throughout life.
11–20	Glandular secretions	Oil and sweat glands become more active.
10–17	Growth spurt	The body takes on a new, more muscular and angular shape. Muscle mass and strength increases. The greatest effect can usually be seen in the upper chest and shoulder muscles.

influence, although external factors, such as diet, may contribute to hair production or hair loss.

Another classic sign of puberty in males is the deepening of the voice, a product of elongation of the larynx. Probably all men remember the embarrassment of their voice "cracking" in their early teenage years. Also, the skin becomes more oily, and breakouts become commonplace. Some teens struggle with severe acne as a result. Acne is produced because the puberty hormones signal the sebaceous glands (tiny glands located in the skin) to produce more oil. The oil is necessary to lubricate the skin, but it can clog pores and provides a fertile ground for bacteria to grow, causing the skin to become inflamed. Since the highest numbers of sebaceous glands are situated on the face, chest, shoulders, and back, these areas tend to be where acne is worst. Despite what you may have heard from friends or even adults, pimples are not caused by greasy foods or chocolate. The reproductive hormones also trigger an increase in perspiration and body odor. Sweat glands under the arms begin to produce oil at puberty—as well as ordinary sweat. The oil serves as a food for bacteria; it is the bacteria that causes body odor. Deodorants work by inhibiting the growth of the bacteria.

Biological Changes in Females

Estrogen is the primary hormone for pubertal development in females. Estrogen triggers the development of the primary sex organs—the uterus and ovaries. The hallmark of sexual maturity for girls is the onset of **menstruation**, or the "period." Menstruation results from an incredible combination of hormonal and physical events that take place about once a month to prepare the female body for the possibility of pregnancy. Once a girl begins menstruating, no matter how young, she is capable of getting pregnant.

The outward expression of female maturity stems from the development of secondary sex characteristics. To put it simply, the female body tends to get curvier. The breasts get larger and undergo changes to prepare for nursing a child. The pelvis widens and the distribution of body fat changes. At puberty, females tend to acquire a higher overall percentage of body fat, with concentrations around the hips, thighs, buttocks, and breasts.

Other physical changes that are triggered at puberty are the same in girls as in boys. One of the most common early signs of puberty is darker, coarse hair under the arms and in the pubic area. Girls will also experience an increase in pimples. Some will suffer severe acne. Girls will also begin to experience more intense body odor; however, neither skin breakouts nor

Table 2.2 Stages of Puberty in Girls

Average Age in Years	Features	What Happens
8 2/3	Growth spurt	Height spurt begins. Body fat at 15.7%.
11 1/4	Breasts	The pigmented area around the nipple enlarges and becomes darker. Breast tissue begins to develop.
11 3/4	Pubic hair and growth	A few coarse dark hairs appear near genitalia.
11 2/3	Growth	Peak height velocity (maximum growth rate) is reached. Body fat approaches 21.6%.
12 1/3	Menstruation	Menarche (first menstrual period) occurs in 20% of girls during this stage.
13	Growth	Average end of growth spurt. Body fat reaches mature proportion: 26%.
15 1/4	Breasts	Adult breasts.

body odor is a sign of poor hygiene. The relationship between puberty, pimples, and body odor is described above in the section describing biological changes in males.

COGNITIVE DEVELOPMENT

Another major benchmark of the adolescent period is a shift in cognitive or intellectual processing. A biologist named Jean Piaget has been heralded as one of the most important influences on understanding cognitive development in children. He noted that young children process information differently from older children and adults and use different strategies to solve problems over the course of development. Very young children grasp only the most simplistic concepts (for example, dropping a rubber duck over the edge of the high chair does not make it go away—even if it falls out of sight). Older children are capable of understanding considerably more sophisticated concepts (for example, the volume of milk does not change when it is poured from a short, thick glass into a tall, thin one). Piaget proposed that humans develop thinking skills by organizing experiences and observations into a conceptual framework. Piaget called this an "operation" or a process of figuring something out. Young children do little mental "figuring." Instead they have to try things out; one example is counting on their fingers. Over

The Brain and Precocious Puberty

Precocious (early) puberty occurs when the physical and hormonal signs of sexual development emerge earlier than normal. It is more common in girls than in boys. There is some debate as to when pubertal development should be considered precocious in girls. Some girls may experience breast enlargement and pubic hair growth as early as age 6 but do not menstruate until an "average" age. It has been argued that the definition of normal development should be revised for racial differences. However, some physicians hold that any sign of pubertal development before age 8 in girls is precocious. For boys, the appearance of puberty before 9 years of age is considered precocious. Scientists believe that precocious puberty is caused by an early increase in the levels of gonadotropin-releasing hormone (GnRH), which signals the pituitary gland to begin time children begin to learn to figure out more things in their head. At about the onset of puberty, children begin the final and most advanced stage of cognitive development. Piaget described this final stage as the *formal operations.*

During the formal operations stage, adolescents begin to think abstractly. They can take a problem and think it over the way a scientist might, considering different variables in the problem and how changing any one variable, or a combination of them, might affect the outcome. At this stage, adolescents also develop the ability to draw generalized conclusions from conditions or situations that are very specific. For example, as a child, Taryn felt terribly sad when her friend Camille's uncle died in a military conflict in the Middle East. However, it was several years later, when Taryn was a teen, before she understood that

the sequence of sexual development earlier than normal. There likely is an assortment of triggers for the premature upregulation of GnRH, but the process is poorly understood. Precocious puberty can be halted by giving medication that blocks the action of the GnRH. The treatment is stopped at the time for normal puberty. There may be several considerations for halting precocious puberty. The early physical and sexual development leads to a large disparity between precocious children and their peers, which can produce embarrassment and a sense of isolation. Behavioral problems are reported in these children, particularly increased aggression in boys. Also, precocious menstruation means girls will be fertile and can become pregnant at very young ages. However, there are no known long-term health problems in children who mature early.

others also felt deep sadness when someone that they cared for died. Her ability to understand what others felt based on her own experiences is an example of making a generalized conclusion based on a specific experience.

During the formal operations stage, adolescents begin to use deductive reasoning, making decisions using hypotheses and ideas rather than just physical facts. Also at puberty, young people become concerned with the future and with ideological problems. A typical example is Betsy, who at about the age of 13 became consumed with imagining every conceivable variable that could enter a situation. That way, she could make plans for how she would handle any of the possible events that could occur. Betsy's mother grumbled that, for a while, Betsy's favorite comeback always began with, "But what if …" For example, when her Dad stated that he did not think young teen girls (such as his daughter) should go on dates with older boys, Betsy countered with, "But what if he was just driving me to the dance?" She did not have plans for an older boy to take her to the dance, but she wanted to know what would happen if the opportunity presented itself. Once her Dad gave his opinion of that scenario, Betsy asked, "But what if we have another couple on the date with us?" and so on until her very frustrated dad threw up his hands and said he would consider reasonable exceptions only when they occurred.

Often, the standards and values young people adopt closely resemble those they were raised with, but, before settling on what they know, adolescents often "try on" different behaviors and viewpoints. In some instances, these exploits bring a sense of panic to parents and may engender considerable strife within a family. However, since the ultimate goal of the adolescent period is to mold young adults who have a healthy self-identity and a strong sense of values (whether or not they match their parents'), the struggle is an important part of growing up.

Not all adolescents go through Piaget's final stage of cognitive development. In fact, some never will. The reason some teens progress through the formal operations stage of cognitive development and others do not is unclear. Scientists have suggested that education helps children develop formal operational thinking. For example, studying lots of science and math in school may foster deductive reasoning and improve abstract thought. Also, certain cultures may place special emphasis on certain types of educational training (such as science and math), so that children in that culture may be more inclined to use the tools (that is, formal operations) that they are taught to value. Finally, not all individuals progress sequentially from a lower to a higher level of cognitive thought. In fact, some may regress, or go from a high level to a lower level, in their cognitive development. Such a regression may indicate emotional disturbances or psychological abnormalities.

EMOTIONAL DEVELOPMENT

Turbulent storms in mood typify society's representation of the adolescent period. Newspapers and magazines depict the typical teen experience as suffused with insecurities, peer pressure, discomfort with one's newly developing body, a struggle for self-identity, and a distrust of elders, particularly parents. The view has been described by psychologists as the turmoil theory of adolescent development. According to the theory, adolescent angst and rebellion are essential and unavoidable, and almost required for the transition from childhood to adulthood. However, there are degrees of turbulence, and most adolescents do not experience the extreme sort that the turmoil theory brings to mind.

It is certainly true that the teenage years can be difficult. Adolescents are discovering the rules of adult ethics, sexuality, and responsibility. They are developing their own values and doing so often involves trying on the fashions and attitudes of their peers. Thus, it is not surprising that most individuals admit to some discouragement and strife during their teen years. However, the majority of teens surveyed report that their families are supportive, they have friendships that they value, and they enjoy a moderate degree of self-confidence. Only a small percentage of teens report more turmoil than contentment during their teenage years.[3] For these teens, there tends to be a strong sense of loneliness and isolation.

Many parents enjoy watching their children transform into adult thinkers. It can be exciting to see young people begin to grapple with the rules of adult morality, and to develop their own value system and code of ethics. That is not to say that parents do not get upset at their teenagers. Thus, it may come as some comfort to parents to know that adolescent moodiness and rebellion may relate to big changes going on in the teenage brain.

■ **Learn more about the contents of this chapter** Search the Internet for *puberty, cognitive development,* and *adolescent development.*

3 Brain Growth and Refinement During Adolescence

The room is pitch black, and Leigh is completely alone. Afraid to move even a finger, she lays on the hard, steel table, crammed inside the belly of a gargantuan machine that grinds and clanks so loudly that Leigh cannot even hear the hammering of her heart. A mass of cold, gray steel is so close to Leigh's face that she is tortured by an inner battle against the all-encompassing claustrophobic panic that threatens. Minutes drag by, seeming like hours. Just as Leigh begins to wonder how much more she can stand of the agonizing immobility, Nurse Cindy opens the door, bustles into the room and chirps, "Now that wasn't so bad, was it?" Leigh's brain scan, using a relatively new technology called **magnetic resonance imaging (MRI)**, is finally complete. The machine is turned off and the noises fade away. Leigh is rolled out of the enormous steel contraption and congratulated on being such a good patient. Leigh has a dread of cramped spaces but the whole process was fascinating—like she was a character in a science fiction movie.

MRI is now a widely used research tool because it provides incredibly accurate, high-resolution images of the brain's anatomy without the use of harmful dyes or radiation. Inside the machine are super-sized magnets that magnetize particles inside the brain, making them jiggle. The energy from the jiggling particles is detected, recorded, and then processed through complex mathematical formulas. Next thing you know, out comes a high-resolution image of Leigh's brain. Because the MRI scans provide much more detail than is possible with any other form of noninvasive imaging technique, the MRI has become an extremely popular tool for diagnosing medical conditions and also for neuroscience research (Figure 3.1).

RECENT STUDIES OF HUMAN BRAIN DEVELOPMENT

One of the most creative uses of MRI technology to help understand brain development is to scan the brains of children several times over the course of years to see whether and how brains change with development. In one particular study, Dr. Jay Giedd and his colleagues at the National Institute of Mental Health created MRI scans of 145 children, some of whom were scanned at 2-year intervals, from preadolescence into early adulthood. Thanks to the willingness of those stalwart kids who volunteered to have their brain scanned repeatedly over the course of years, we now have critical data for understanding how the brain grows.

All earlier studies of brain development relied on averaged measurements from many different children. Typically, the data from all children of a given age were lumped together and brain size or weight was averaged for each age group. This method did not provide the most accurate results, because variability in brain sizes is huge, even for the same age, and large variation within a group tends to confound statistical methods. As a simple example, imagine that three high school seniors are shopping together for their prom dresses. One girl finds her dress in a secondhand store and pays $75. The other two found dresses in a department store and paid $175 and $250 respectively. Their friend, who is writing an article for the school newspaper about the costs of the high school prom, uses the information

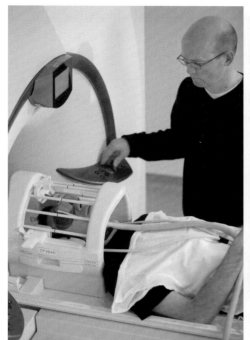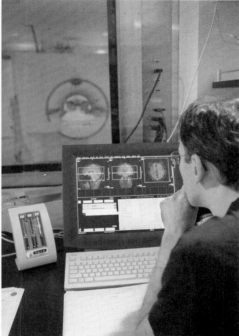

Figure 3.1 Imaging technology allows doctors and researchers to observe the brain without invasive surgery. At left, a patient enters a magnetic resonance imaging machine that will monitor brain activity over a period of seconds to minutes. At right, a scientist views images created by the machine.

from the girls' shopping excursion and reports that the average costs of prom dresses is $166.66. In the meantime, the first girl exchanges her dress for another dress that costs $90, a 20% increase in the amount of money she had to spend for a prom dress. For her, this is a fairly significant increase in expense. However, the impact on the average cost of the three dresses is almost trivial. The new average is $171.66, only a 3% increase from the original. Thus, measurements that rely on averages can be deceptive, and scientists worried that some of the fine details about how the brain grows during development might be lost when data from a large population of children are combined.

Nonetheless, early studies based on measurements from large samples of children were useful for showing overall trends in brain growth during development. For example, the data show that the brain does most of its growing during prenatal and early postnatal development. After the age of 2 or 3 years, brain growth slows considerably. By about 6 years of age, the average brain has reached 90%–95% of its adult size. After that, there is a slight increase in brain size until the early twenties, and then, over the course of the next 5 to 6 decades, average brains have a very small decline in size (Figure 3.2).

Another problem with earlier studies of brain growth was that measurements usually included the entire brain (brain weight or mass) or the whole head (head circumference). Yet the brain is composed of many different parts. For example, the **gray matter** contains large numbers of **neurons**, or nerve cells, which are responsible for processing electrical activity (the neural signals) in the brain (Figure 3.3). Gray matter also contains **glia** (brain cells that have multiple roles to support neurons but that do not transmit neural signals). The **white matter** is composed of large numbers of **axons**, the long fiberlike extensions that transmit the electrical activity generated by nerve cells. Deep inside the brain are **ventricles**, spaces filled with cerebrospinal fluid, that transport products to (such as hormones) and from (such as waste products) the brain. So, measurements that include the whole brain could not resolve details about how each of the different parts of the brain grows.

Imagine trying to figure out what was in a bunch of backpacks by simply looking at them piled up on the gym floor. Backpacks of all colors and styles will be in the pile, and some probably will be decorated with ribbons, artwork, or other personal identifiers. Some backpacks will be big, and others will be moderately sized. If you were asked to hypothesize about what was inside just by looking at the backpacks in the pile, the best

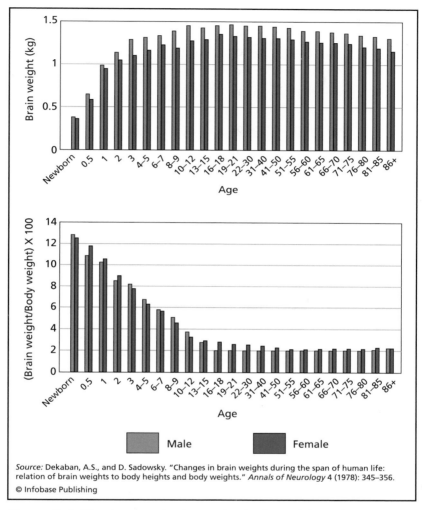

Figure 3.2 The top graph shows the brain weights of males and females at different ages. The bottom graph shows the brain weight to total body weight ratio (expressed as a percentage). The adult brain makes up approximately 2% of the total body weight, whereas a newborn's brain makes up approximately 13% of the total weight.

you could do would be to predict that the big backpacks would contain more books, folders, and possibly gym clothes than the smaller ones. You certainly could not tell which contained a

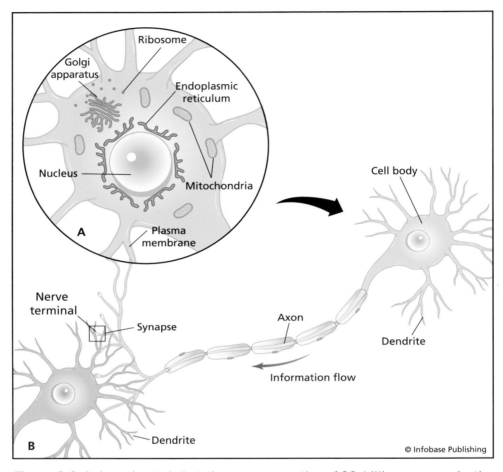

Figure 3.3 It is estimated that there are more than 100 billion neurons in the human brain. (A) Neurons, like all cells, contain specialized components known as organelles. (B) Electrical signals travel down the axon of a neuron toward the dendrite of an adjacent neuron. The junction between the two neurons is called a synapse.

chemistry textbook and which held an iPod. You would simply have to guess. Scientists who tried to make guesses about brain growth by just looking at head size or overall brain weight had the same difficulties.

What Giedd and his coworkers discovered was that the brain was developing in very interesting ways between the ages of about 6 years to the early twenties. They found that despite what seems like an almost trivial growth in overall size, the brain was undergoing considerable resculpting during this time. Moreover, different parts of the brain had very different developmental trajectories. For example, the ventricles and white matter grow slowly but steadily in a nearly linear fashion that mirrors the findings taken from average brain weights. However, the gray matter develops differently. The dissimilarity is particularly notable in the **cerebral cortex**, the sheet of gray matter that forms the outer covering of the brain. The cortical gray matter has a wave of new growth followed by a progressive thinning and overall reduction in cortical volume.

Perhaps the most important discovery from the study by Giedd and his colleagues is that different regions of cerebral cortex mature at different ages. For instance, cortical areas that oversee some of our more fundamental behaviors, such as sensation and perception, have a relatively early growth surge. In these areas, the volume of cortex peaks at about 8.5 years of age and then thins subsequently as maturation continues. Cortex in the **frontal lobe** (Figure 3.4), which oversees motor coordination, regulates attention and orchestrates behavior, has a later growth surge. In this region, cortical size crests between the ages of 11 and 12, and then thinning and refinement occurs. Next to proceed through these developmental sequences are parts of the **temporal lobes**, which peak at about the age of 16 years. Cortex in the temporal lobes has a variety of functions that include the integration of memory, ability to recognize objects, and speech processing. The last cortical region to go through the growth surge and subsequent refinement is **prefrontal cortex** (the portion of the frontal lobe closest to the forehead), which does not reach adult dimensions until the early twenties.

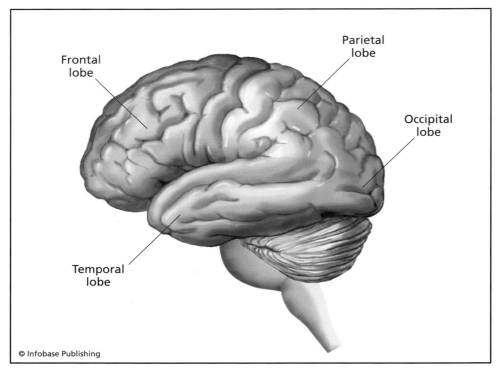

Figure 3.4 The cerebral cortex consists of four sections, or lobes. Functions of the body, such as vision, speech, and movement, can often be pinpointed to specific locations within the lobes.

Much has been made of this finding of the delayed development of prefrontal cortex. Prefrontal cortex is responsible for planning and decision making, and is often called the CEO (chief executive officer) of the brain. The fact that it is growing and remodeling throughout the teenage years suggests that the teen brain is functioning without its executive "override," the little voice of caution that keeps us from reacting impulsively. As we will see in Chapter 6, new research suggests that decision making by teens tends to be impulsive and inclined toward immediate gratification. This may reflect the underdevelopment of the prefrontal cortex.

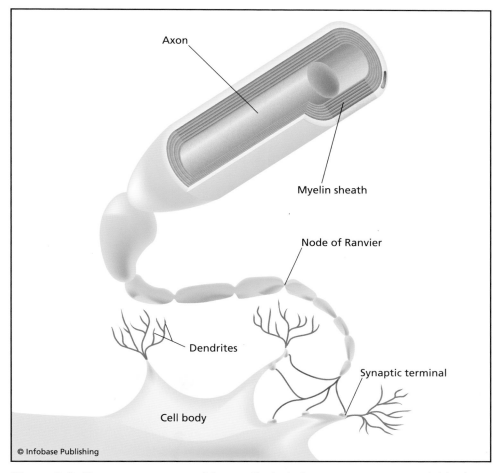

Figure 3.5 Neurons are wrapped in myelin to help messages move quickly down the axon.

Now let's switch gears and briefly consider the development of other aspects of the nervous system. As mentioned earlier, the white matter, consisting of the axons that carry information from one cell to another, grows steadily bigger and bigger during development. This growth probably reflects the development of protective sheaths covering individual axons. The protective covering is called **myelin** (Figure 3.5).

Table 3.1 Roles of Various Brain Structures

STRUCTURE	DESCRIPTION / DUTIES
Corpus Callosum	The bundle of nerve fibers connects the left and right hemispheres of the brain. During adolescence, the nerve fibers thicken and process information more and more efficiently.
Prefrontal Cortex	The CEO of the brain is one of the last parts of the brain to mature, which may be why teens get into so much trouble.
Basal Ganglia	The basal ganglia and prefrontal cortex are tightly connected; at nearly the same time, they grow neuron connections and then prune them.
Amygdala	This is the emotional center of the brain, home to such primal feelings as fear and rage. It grows during childhood and adolescence, and functions in an adult-like way earlier than prefrontal cortex. Since the prefrontal cortex monitors our emotional tendencies, the different maturation rates may explain why adolescents react more emotionally than adults.
Cerebellum	Long thought to play a role in physical coordination, this area may also support higher thought processes like mathematics, music, and advanced social skills. The cerebellum continues growing well into the early twenties.

Source: Claudia Wallis and Kristina Dell, with reporting by Alice Park. "What Makes Teens Tick." *Time* (May 10, 2004).

Myelin is produced by special cells in the brain (a certain type of glia) whose job is to support neurons. Glia send out processes that wrap around an axon many times; the wrapping itself is what is called myelin. Not only does myelin provide structural support for axons, it also greatly increases the speed at which neuronal information (the electrical impulse) is passed through an axon. In the absence of myelin, electrical impulses flow down an axon in a wave-like form. In the presence of myelin, the electrical signal skips along the axon at an incredibly high

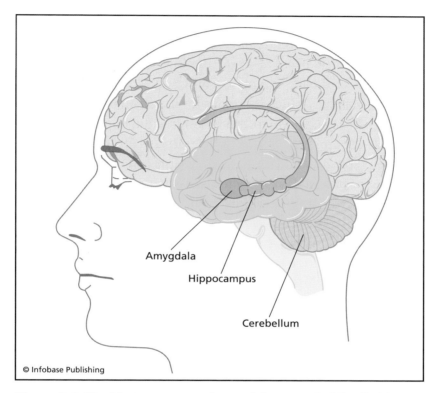

© Infobase Publishing

Figure 3.6 The hippocampus and amygdala are part of the limbic system, which is involved in the expression of emotions. The cerebellum is responsible for the coordination of movement and balance.

rate of speed. A trip from one side of the brain to the other, through the **corpus callosum** which connects the left and right halves of the brain, might take only a fraction of a second for an unmyelinated axon, but compared to the time it would take a myelinated fibers to send information over the same distance, it is downright slow. To put it in real numbers, unmyelinated axons transmit the neural signal at a maximum speed of about 4.5 miles per hour (7.2 kilometers per hour). In contrast, large myelinated axons can relay the information at about 270 miles per hour (435 km/h).

Regions of the brain other than cerebral cortex also show interesting growth trends during adolescent development. The **amygdala,** which processes information about emotion, has a growth spurt during childhood and adolescence (Figure 3.6). The **hippocampus,** which is famous for its role in memory formation and storage, also increases in volume during the same time frame as the amygdala. Conversely, portions of the **basal ganglia** that help control and execute movements lose volume at about the time of puberty. Finally, the **cerebellum**, which is involved in a wide assortment of behaviors, continues growing well after the end of adolescence. The cerebellum has classically been known for maintaining posture and equilibrium, and for motor learning. More recently it also has been implicated in higher brain functions, including the processing of language and music, and for directing attention. Scientists are still puzzled by what the late growth of the cerebellum might mean for adolescents.

EXUBERANT BRAIN GROWTH FOLLOWED BY REFINEMENT

The surge of new growth in the cerebral cortex that has been observed during the adolescent years is followed by a progressive thinning and overall reduction in cortical volume. Scientists have speculated that this cortical thinning may be just as important, if not more so, than the preceding surge in cortical growth. Imagine that you have piled all your clothes on your bed—clothes from every corner of your closet, from all drawers, even from under your bed. That might be a big pile, especially if you have not been forced to cull out things that you have outgrown in the past few years. Now imagine that you remove all the tops, bottoms, sock, shoes, and underwear that you have outgrown or do not like, and donate it to charity. The pile of clothes on the bed will have gotten smaller (for some, it may be much, much smaller). Yet the loss will not have any impact on your attire.

Your favorite clothes and all the stuff that you need will still be there. In fact, since you will have fewer things to sort through, the process of choosing an outfit might become more efficient.

The same principle applies to the developing brain. The brain accumulates more cells and **synapses** (where neural signals are passed between nerve cells) than it needs. This is called "exuberant" growth in the brain. Then over time and after much mental exercise, there is selective elimination of some cells and synapses. Scientists believe that this process of selective elimination of cells and connections creates a more efficient brain.

The process is much like the natural pruning of leaves and branches on a tree. Leaves that get insufficient sunlight fail to thrive and their connecting branch grows weak. Eventually, the branch may die, and in cases of extremely limited sunlight (such as under a dense forest canopy), the whole tree may perish. In contrast, leaves that get lots of sunlight flourish, their branches get bigger and make more leaves, and the tree thrives. In a competitive environment, this sort of process can be highly advantageous for the population. Weak trees are susceptible to disease and insects, which can spread to the strong trees nearby, and ultimately the whole forest can be compromised.

It is much the same in the nervous system, following a process dubbed as "use it or lose it." Cells that get sufficient neural activation grow bigger and extend longer, more complex dendrites, the nerve extensions where many of the synapses are located. Existing synapses get bigger, and additional synapses are formed. In general, active neurons flourish. At the other end of the spectrum, neurons that do not receive sufficient synaptic activation lose synapses. If enough synapses on a dendritic process are lost, the entire dendrite may vanish. Whole neurons may even die. Over time, the brain is whittled down so that only neurons and synaptic connections that get used, and presumably contribute to brain function, are retained.

CRITICAL PERIODS OF BRAIN DEVELOPMENT

So bigger is not necessarily better in neuroscience. But, if that is the case, why has the evidence for a surge of new growth near adolescence caused such a stir among scientists? For decades, our understanding of the developing brain was that the **critical period** for brain development (the time when most brain growth and refinement takes place) is during the first 3 years

Critical Period for Language

A critical period during development is a restricted period of time during which normal experience is essential for achieving proficiency at the task. One of the best known critical periods for humans involves language. Exposure to normal language before the age of 7 years is essential for a child to achieve a thorough command of the language. After that, the degree of language proficiency that can be achieved diminishes. Children rescued from abusive households where there is no exposure to language have difficulty mastering even a primary language if the rescue does not occur until after the age of 7. However, hearing the language spoken is not essential. Instead, it is the process of communication that seems to be most essential. Congenitally deaf children who are taught sign language can develop as many advanced language skills as children with normal hearing. Learning a second language also is dictated by this critical period. Thus a child who begins to learn a second language before the age of 7 can develop even the most subtle aspects of the second language, including speech sounds and rules of grammar. However, an individual who begins learning a second language after the age of 7 may acquire a large vocabulary in the second language but may never achieve full proficiency.

of life. Some scientists even had gone so far as to state that all the machinery of the brain (nerve cells and all their connections) was in place by about 10 years of age. We now know that that is not true. In fact, small changes in neuronal wiring are possible throughout life, accompanying learning and recovery from injury. However, during a period of intense growth and refinement, there is a much better opportunity to improve brain function, or to put it another way, to be as smart as you can be. So scientists are now viewing the adolescent period not only as a time of immense hormonal and physical flux, but also as a critical time for brain development and for optimizing the brain's potential.

■ **Learn more about the contents of this chapter** Search the Internet for *brain development*, *brain imaging*, and *critical period*.

4 | Training the Brain

Standing 5'10" and weighing 140 pounds, Sam was big for someone in the seventh grade. Not surprisingly, the football coach at his junior high school was Sam's number one fan, and that suited Sam just fine because he liked to tackle. However, Sam's secret goal was to be good in basketball as well. Tyrone, his uncle, had been a star on the high school basketball team. He went on to play for the University of Tennessee and then played professional basketball for 6 years. Sam wanted to play basketball like Tyrone.

There was one catch to Sam's hopes. He was strongly right-hand dominant and was vulnerable when guarded on his weak (left) side. Tyrone knew that if Sam wanted to be the best basketball player that he could be, he needed to develop his weak-hand dribbling and shooting. Tyrone had just the tool to help him learn.

Since leaving professional basketball, Tyrone had devoted himself to helping young basketball players refine their skills. At 6'7" and 250 pounds, Tyrone could be an intimidating presence, but because of his easy laugh and his compassionate manner, kids responded well to him and typically would try their hardest. However, time and again, he struggled to teach kids how to develop their weak side game. The worst was the running left-handed layup. (For left-hand–dominant players, the challenge would be the running right-handed layup.)

"It's the footwork." Tyrone lamented, "They just can't get it!" So he developed a brilliant tool, called The Layup Master. It is a simple mat that indicates which foot to place where as the player approaches the basket from his or her weak side.

Tyrone brought The Layup Master to Sam and showed him how to use it. Sam struggled mightily with the first few tries. Eventually he learned how to walk to the basket, placing his feet correctly on the mat so that he could spring from his dominant foot to shoot with his nondominant hand. Running to the basket and placing the feet in the correct positions were considerably more difficult, but Sam refused to give up. He practiced for the remainder of the afternoon, even missed dinner with the family because he was determined to learn. When he finally quit for the night, after hundreds of tries, Sam had developed his running left-handed layup. It took many, many more practice shots before Sam could move to the basket for a left-handed lay-up with the innate sense that he needed, so that he did not falter under pressure when the game was on the line. Now, as a starting player on his high school team, Sam has all the tools he needs to follow in his uncle's footsteps.

Although Sam was not aware of changes taking place in his brain, that is exactly what happened. Sam had repeated the series of movements needed to make the shot so many times that he literally trained circuits in his brain. The modified circuits could send signals to his limbs in the appropriate sequence so that he could perform the difficult combination of footsteps and hand movements needed to execute the shot. The scientific term for modification in the brain is **plasticity** (the ability of a structure in the brain to change shape or function).

CHANGES IN BRAIN FUNCTION

Neuroplasticity refers to processes that allow for changes in brain organization and in brain activity. A powerful driving force for plasticity is neuronal activity—the tiny electrical signals that

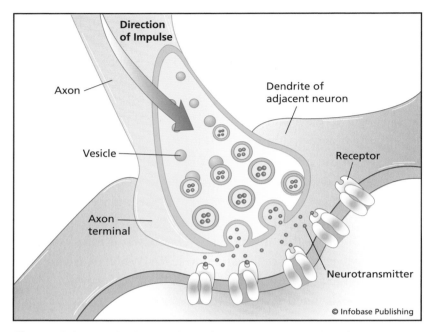

Figure 4.1 In this illustration of a synapse, an electrical impulse causes the release of neurotransmitters from vesicles within the neuron. The neurotransmitters then bind to receptors of an adjacent neuron. When a neurotransmitter binds to a receptor, it may result in a new impulse generated by the postsynaptic (receiving) neuron, or it may serve to inhibit the firing of an impulse.

are generated by cells (neurons) in the brain (Figure 4.1). The very simplest example of the effects of neuronal activity on nerve cells is **long-term potentiation**, known as LTP. LTP was first discovered by scientists looking for ways to explain short-term memory. Early scientists assumed that the brain was not capable of change, at least not after the brain had gone through the early critical period of development. Therefore, they reasoned that new memories could not be explained by physical changes in the brain, but instead probably resulted from modifications in the electrical properties, the **synaptic activity**, of individual brain cells.

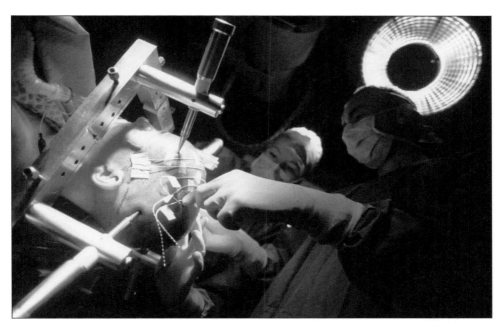

Figure 4.2 In this photograph, a surgeon implants electrodes into a patient's brain in order to record the electrical activity of neurons.

Scientists discovered LTP using **electrophysiological** techniques, which reveal the synaptic activity of neurons (Figure 4.2). An extremely fine electrode is inserted into the region of the brain being studied. Electrodes can detect the small electrical currents generated in the cell bodies of neurons. Because the currents generated by brain cells are tiny, the electrical signals must be amplified many times so that it can be observed, much like turning up the volume on a car stereo loudly enough for everyone in surrounding vehicles to hear the music.

With modern technology, the electrode can be positioned very precisely in the brain and moved in steps as small as one micron (about the size of the tip of a hair). As the electrode is lowered through the region of the brain to be studied, the scientist monitors the amplified activity relayed from the electrode and looks for patterns of electrical activity that are typical of neurons. Briskly active neurons make a distinctive snap, crackle, and pop that grows louder as the tip of the electrode is moved closer. Once the tip of the electrode is near enough to pick up strong signals from one or a small number of cells, the scientist begins to collect information. Electrical pulses produced by neurons can be analyzed in every conceivable fashion, including counting and timing spikes in the electrical current and measuring the heights of the spikes. If a neuron is strongly activated by a stimulus, it typically will respond by producing many, tall spikes in a very short period of time. A weak stimulus usually will cause the cell to emit fewer spikes, which may also be much shorter in height.

When LTP was discovered, the activity of neurons was being recorded in the hippocampus (known to be associated with memory). The procedure was to record the electrical current in the hippocampus that was produced by stimulating the neurons that connect to the hippocampus. To stimulate the connecting neurons, a tiny electric shock was given to their processes at a location far away from the hippocampus. The shock triggered an electrical response, called an **action potential**, that raced all the way to the hippocampus and activated new electrical currents inside the hippocampal neurons. Each time a shock was given to the connecting neurons, cells in the hippocampus generated a very clear-cut electrical response. The response of the hippocampal neurons was exactly the same every time the shock was delivered. Inadvertently during the experiment, a much stronger stimulus was delivered so that the connecting neurons received a series of multiple shocks. Incredibly, for quite a long time after the series of shocks when the same single stimulus as used originally was delivered, the hippocampal neurons responded much more strongly than ever before. The discovery was incredibly exciting in the neuroscience community. It was proof that the electrical properties of nerve cells can be molded by incoming information, and signal new events to their downstream partners in a brain circuit.

CHANGES IN BRAIN STRUCTURE

Brain activity also is an important force for changes to the structure of the brain, including the size, shape, and even chemical makeup of brain cells. Some of the earliest evidence that brain size and organization can be modified came from studies where young rats were raised in cages packed with an assortment of rat "toys," such as an exercise wheel, parallel bar, and items to sniff and gnaw. Usually laboratory rats are housed in fairly simple cages, and in those cages, rats do little except eat and sleep. In contrast, rats raised with plenty of toys spend time puttering around their cages, exploring the toys.

After several weeks spent in the more complex environment, the brains of the rats were compared to the brains of rats of the same age that lived in standard cages. The experimental rats had significantly larger brains. Even individual brain cells were different, with larger **dendritic fields,** the weblike network of processes that extends from the neuron to receive synaptic input. Most importantly, the rats that lived in the complex environments were faster at figuring out rat mazes than typical laboratory rats, so it was assumed that larger brains helped the rats perform better.

Dr. William Greenough and his colleagues at the Beckman Institute, University of Illinois, collected much of the data about the effects of complex environments on nerve cell structure. They argue that what we might view as a "complex" environment in a laboratory setting may be no richer for a rat than living in the wild, where there are trashcans to explore and predators to evade. If that's the case, then the brains of the rats from the complex environments probably are not super-sized. Instead, what might be happening in the standard laboratory setting is that, because of a lack of stimulation provided rats in standard cages, their brain growth and development might be stunted.

Because scientists assumed that the brains of adults were hardwired (so that memories and learned behaviors, such as walking, could be preserved), the early studies of the effects of housing rats in complex environments were performed in young rats. However, Dr. Greenough and his coworkers found that the brains of adult rats also grew larger after living in cages equipped with exercise equipment and novelties. The increase in brain size was less impressive than it was in the young rats, but the effect was unequivocal. Adult brain cells that were more active can produce larger dendritic fields and have increased synaptic numbers compared to their less active counterparts.

This evidence of plasticity in the adult brain made perfect sense. After all, if the adult brain was incapable of change, how could we explain the seemingly miraculous recoveries of individuals following head injury? In fact, adult plasticity now has been shown in nearly all parts of the brain and under a wide assortment of circumstances.

BRAIN PLASTICITY AND CHANGES IN BEHAVIORAL CAPACITY

Even with all this evidence, who really cares whether nerve cells get bigger and give stronger responses after a series of shocks? These would only be neat factoids if the changes have no influence on how the brain works. But how is it possible to learn anything about what the whole brain, consisting of billions of neurons, is doing by performing experiments on only a small sample of cells? Dr. Michael Merzenich and his colleagues at the Keck Center for Integrative Neurosciences at the University of California at San Francisco came up with an ingenious way to investigate the question.

For their study, Dr. Merzenich and his team first trained monkeys to report when they felt a difference in the rate of tapping applied to one of their hands. The monkeys were relatively tame, and they had been taught to sit and hold one hand very still in a hand mold made especially for each monkey. Then, a series of rapid taps, a vibration, was applied through the mold to a specific part of the hand (for example, to the middle portion of the index finger). Immediately afterward, a second, different vibration was applied to the same part of the hand.

The test for the monkey was to decide if the second vibration differed in frequency from the first. If the vibrations were judged to be different, the monkey removed his hand from the mold and got a treat. The same experiment was performed over and over again, always with the vibration applied to the same, small part of the hand. With practice, the monkeys became good at detecting the differences in vibration frequencies.

A neat twist to the experiment was that the vibration was not applied to the same part of the hand in each of the monkeys. In some monkeys, the vibration was applied to the middle portion of the index finger, in others the vibration was applied to the tip of the index finger, and in yet other monkeys, the vibration was applied to a part of the long finger. In every case, the monkey's improvements in distinguishing vibration were specific to the area of the finger that was repeatedly stimulated. If the vibration was applied to other skin areas, the monkey was not as good at the task. In other words, the monkey did not simply learn how to do the task better. Instead, increased sensory stimulation to a portion of the hand made only that particular part of the hand better at sensing the differences in vibration.

Next, Dr. Merzenich and his colleagues examined the region of the brain used to feel the differences in vibration frequencies. Their goal was to discover whether the extensive training had caused changes in brain organization. Using electrophysiological procedures, the scientists recorded the activity of neurons in the part of the brain responsible for sensing vibration. In this particular brain region, cells are exquisitely sensitive to vibration applied to only a very small part of the body surface. Therefore, only a cluster of neurons are dedicated to sensing vibration to the thumb, an adjacent cluster is devoted to sensing vibration on the index finger, and so on. By studying many neurons, it is possible to generate a "neuronal map" that senses vibration to the body surface. Dr. Merzenich and his research team discovered that the representation of the hand in the brain had changed as a result of the extensive training that the monkeys had received. For each animal, the region of the brain devoted to the small skin area that

Hebb's Rule

In 1949, Professor Donald Hebb speculated that there must be basic "rules" that guide brain behavior in all species. He came to his conclusions simply by observing how the behavior of an organism was affected by disturbances in the brain. His early experiments involved visual tests on rats with disrupted visual pathways. In later studies he tested memory and intelligence in humans with brain injury.

What has come to be known as Hebb's rule is: If the electrical activity in two neighboring neurons is closely correlated, then the connections between those same neurons will strengthen. In simpler terms: *cells that fire together, wire together.* Over the course of time, Hebb's rule has been confirmed using different experimental approaches, in different brain structures and in different species. Hebb's rule was one of the most important conceptual breakthroughs in neuroscience.

had received the vibratory stimulation was bigger than the same region on the other side of the brain (related to the opposite hand that had not been used to detect differences in vibration). The conclusion from this study is that relatively dramatic changes in brain organization, mirrored by improvements in performance, can be produced by repeated practice.

HUMAN BRAIN PLASTICITY

One final question about brain plasticity remains. Even though the findings from the animal experiments are interpreted as important for understanding brain function, just how applicable are they to humans? One team of scientists conceived of a clever way to find out. They realized that blind individuals who "read" using the Braille technique nearly always read with the index finger of the dominant hand—for most of us, our right hand. Proficient Braille readers typically use the procedure daily for 5 to 10 hours, so the reading finger receives intensive sensory stimulation compared to the index finger on the opposite hand. The group invited Braille readers to participate in a brain imaging study. The scientists used procedures that reveal crude maps of brain organization by recording brain activity from electrodes placed on the scalp. The findings were dramatic, and exactly what was predicted from the study on monkeys by Merzenich's group. The area of the brain related to the Braille-reading finger was considerably larger than the same finger on the opposite hand. Specific details about the reorganized brain maps could not be detected, because the technology used in the experiment on Braille readers provided only low resolution images of brain organization, particularly when compared to the incredibly detailed accuracy provided by electrophysiological studies. However, new and improved brain imaging equipment has emerged, and there is little doubt among scientists that evidence for brain plasticity in humans will continue to grow.

CONCLUSIONS

Evidence from research about brain plasticity implies that altera-
tions in brain organization, produced by training, make the
individual better at whatever task has been practiced extensively.
In fact, many scientists assume that neuroplasticity is associated
with the acquisition of new knowledge. However, does this mean
that, with training, an individual with only average intelligence
can become a genius? Probably not. Genetic contributions from
biological parents have a strong influence on the intellectual

Nature Versus Nurture

Evidence for neuroplasticity has had a profound impact on the
debate about whether our inherited qualities ("nature") are
more important than our personal experiences ("nurture") in
determining who we are. The notion that a rich sensory environment early in life might be correlated with bigger brains has
produced a dramatic shift in favor of "nurture" as essential in
brain development. Expectant mothers play classical music
and read poetry to their unborn infants. Toys for infants are
marketed with promises to increase a child's learning capacity,
stimulate the senses, and build confidence. Yet the benefits of
such strategies are disputed. What's more, it would be mislead-
ing to say that genetic inheritance is of no importance for brain
development. As an example, in some strains of Siamese cats
misdirected connections in the visual pathways of the brain
are caused by the same genetic permutation that produces the
pale blue eyes and the distinctively colored fur of Siamese cats.
Thus, although debate continues to rage, scientists generally
agree that there is a complex interaction between genetics and
environmental influences on brain development.

potential of the offspring. Therefore, there are limits to what can be achieved. Also, training can be overdone and even have detrimental consequences. For example, a syndrome called dystonia, which involves involuntary muscle contractions that can be enormously painful, has been found in concert musicians (such as violinists) who practice their musical instrument excessively. The dystonia is attributed to abnormalities in brain function that resulted from the inordinate amount of practice. So, the old saying, "all things in moderation" is a good rule of thumb for learning and brain training.

Perhaps a more realistic interpretation of the evidence for brain plasticity is that, with nurturing and with lots of mental, physical, and emotional experience, the brain's machinery can become more efficient, be less vulnerable to insults such as stress and illness, and possibly retain more information. What's more, since the teen brain is a work in progress, care and handling of the stuff between the ears may be all the more critical.

Finally, although the focus of this chapter is on changes in brain organization that are advantageous, neglect also can alter brain structure and function. In fact, lack of brain stimulation can have the opposite effects as brain training. Neurons may lose synaptic connections, circuits that are not reinforced may be lost and the size of brain territory devoted to a particular task might shrink. In other words, use it or lose it.

■ **Learn more about the contents of this chapter** Search the Internet for *brain plasticity*, *brain enrichment*, and *nature versus nurture*.

5 | The Reward Circuit and Thrill Seeking

Jeremy had his priorities perfectly balanced—for a 16 year old. He was a serious student with all A's and B's on his report card, he devoted himself to football, and during the off-season he worked at a nearby fast food restaurant to make money for college. However, he loved nothing better than a good prank or a bit of mischief. During his junior year in high school, he came up with a list of "accomplishments" that he wanted to achieve before graduation. To the delight of his friends, the list included the goal of successfully driving his car down a notoriously steep and curvy road near his home, without putting on the brakes.

Jeremy had an old Pontiac that he had bought for himself. The car was heavy so it gathered considerable speed on the way down the hill. Also, it had a loose and wobbly suspension. On several occasions when he came to the series of sharp curves near the bottom of the hill going too fast, Jeremy felt certain that the car was going to roll over. Inevitably, he lost his resolve and tapped the brakes. Finally, in his senior year and with two of his friends in the old Pontiac, he made it down the hill around all the curves without ever touching the brakes.

The next day Jeremy proudly described the adventure to the mother of one of the friends who was in the car during the stunt. She gasped as Jeremy described the bucking of the car on the last few curves and pointed out that the stunt was downright dangerous—not just for the kids but also for the families who lived on the street. Without a pause, Jeremy assured his friend's mother that he would never do something that was *seriously* risky. The mother, of course, was alarmed.

Jeremy's answer suggested that the circuitry in Jeremy's brain that is critical for evaluating risk may not have been fully mature yet. In other words, he may not be a good judge of what constitutes a serious risk. The adult brain is very good at processing information about the consequences of risks, the potential for reward and using the information in making decisions. New research suggests that the adolescent brain reacts differently when evaluating risk and reward, and the differences might explain why teens tend to be such risk takers. Before we consider the research data, let's get to know the parts of the brain that are involved.

REWARD CIRCUIT

The primary job of the reward circuit in the brain is to reinforce behaviors that are important for survival. Cells in the reward circuit are activated when we accomplish basic, but vital, tasks such as eating when hungry or drinking when thirsty. This activation produces intense feelings of pleasure, or "reward," and makes us want to repeat the behavior.

The reward circuit consists of specialized compartments in multiple regions of the brain that are interconnected by long-reaching nerve fiber bundles (Figure 5.1). Deep in the brain stem is the **ventral tegmental area (VTA)** which is loaded with neurons that produce the neurotransmitter **dopamine**, which is associated with reward and pleasure. Neurons in the VTA are strongly interconnected with neurons in the **nucleus accumbens**, a structure that processes information about

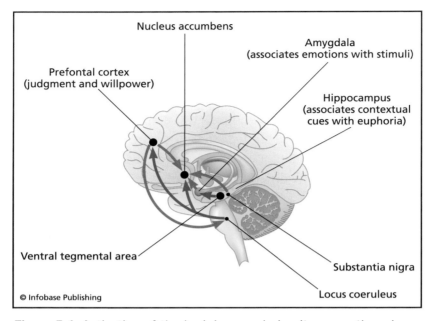

Figure 5.1 Activation of the brain's reward circuit causes the release of the neurotransmitter dopamine from neurons of the ventral tegmental area. Depicted here are the basic reward pathways from the ventral tegmental area to the nucleus accumbens, prefrontal cortex, and amygdala.

emotional state. Both of these structures connect with cells in the prefrontal cortex, an area responsible for higher cognitive functions. Together these structures are responsible for analyzing information that enters the brain to determine whether there is a possibility of a reward being received or a pleasurable event occurring.

In the brains of more primitive animals, this pleasure circuit will facilitate behaviors that lead to immediate reward or pleasure unless there is knowledge of imminent danger or risk. However, in animals with "higher" intellectual function, the possible choices extend far beyond just sorting good from bad. We frequently are given opportunities to choose between better and best. Also, many decisions must factor in variables that may span long periods of time in order to plan strategies to achieve long-term goals. Such sophisticated thought processes involve the prefrontal cortex, which will be discussed in considerable detail in the next chapter.

The idea that stimulation of reward circuits is pleasurable came initially from experimental studies in rats. Ultrafine simulating electrodes were surgically implanted in regions of the rat brains that had been implicated in the reward circuit. Then the rats were trained to press a lever that would send a small electrical pulse through the electrode into the reward system (Figure 5.2). If, as expected, the stimulation mimicked the sensation produced by a reward, then the rat might be inclined to repeat the bar press. On the other hand, if the stimulation produced a noxious sensation, or even just a neutral experience, then the rat would either avoid the bar or show it no special preference. The results were more dramatic than the scientists could have imagined. The rats would press the lever at exceedingly high rates (thousands of times an hour) to receive the electrical activation. What's more, they seemed to prefer the stimulation over any other enticement, including food and water—even after many hours without nourishment.

Areas of the human brain presumed to be reward areas also have been stimulated directly with electrical current. These cases usually involved neurosurgical exploration to identify and remove brain regions suspected of triggering incurable seizures. In this procedure, the scalp, skull and the **meninges** (tough three-layered sheath that covers the brain) are opened surgically in the anesthetized patient. The wound is treated with a long-acting numbing agent, and then the patient is allowed to wake up. Because the brain itself has no sensory nerve endings, the patient does not feel anything during the procedure. As the surgeon sends small electrical pulses into the brain, the patient reports any sensations that are triggered. During the course of this surgery, patients reported feeling

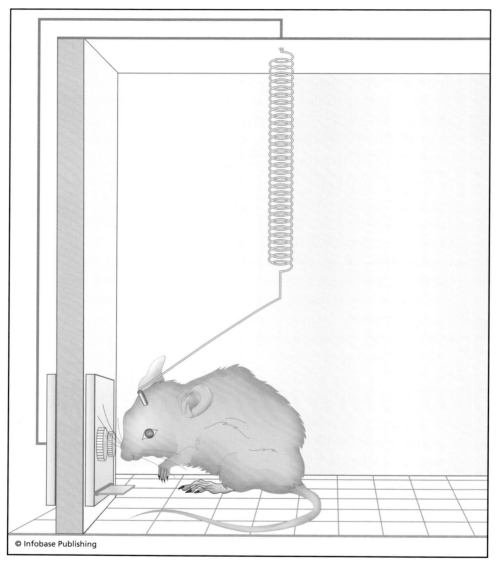

Figure 5.2 This drawing depicts a rat in a self-stimulation chamber. Rats learn by trial and error to press the small metal lever, shown just below the rat's nose. When the lever is pressed, a tiny volt of electric current is passed through an electrode implanted in the brain's reward circuit. The experience is assumed to be pleasurable because rats will press the lever repeatedly, even to the exclusion of food and water.

touches, tickles or tingles, smelled nonexistent odors, made spontaneous movements, and even recalled long-ago memories. When the stimulation encroached on brain regions associated with the reward circuit, the patients reported feelings that were described as intensely pleasurable, even sexual. In fact, one anecdote described a patient developing strong romantic feelings for the surgeon performing the experiment!

Early experiments referred to the region as a reward "center," because the reward-like effects that they saw were produced when one electrode was used to stimulate the brain. It was assumed that a reward region must be located near the tip of the electrode at that one location in the brain. Later, scientists concluded that the stimulation probably activated neurons in additional regions of the brain through long-distance connections that make up a circuit. Thus it came as no surprise when MRI studies of the parts of the brain that process information about potential rewards showed widely distributed activation involving multiple areas of the nervous system. The consequence is that most recent literature refers to the reward system as a circuit, whereas early papers held to the term of a reward center. Some even have dubbed this pathway the "pleasure" center or circuit, which never fails to fascinate even those who are completely bored by science.

The reward circuit reinforces many more behaviors than just eating and drinking. Recent experiments demonstrate that the reward system also mediates feelings of romantic love and attraction. The experiments used a relatively new application of the MRI brain scanner (called functional MRI or fMRI) to reveal differences in levels of activity in the brain. The basic assumption is that regions of the brain that are strongly active during a particular mental task, or when a specific memory or sensation is evoked, are important for that behavior. In the experiment to evaluate the relationship between romantic love and the reward system, the brains of individuals who reported to be in an intense romantic relationship were scanned using fMRI while the individuals alternately looked at a picture of their beloved and of a close acquaintance. Not surprisingly, high levels of activity were present in the reward circuit when the individuals viewed pictures of their beloved. What's more, the activation of the reward system was greatest in individuals who rated their degree of romantic love the highest. In all cases, there was significantly less activation of the reward circuit when the individuals viewed pictures of mere acquaintances.

In another experiment, male subjects (who described themselves as heterosexuals) were asked to view a series of pictures of individuals unknown to them and then rate the people according to beauty. Later, the subjects were asked to view the same pictures while their brains were being scanned using the fMRI procedure. While the men were viewing pictures of women who they had previously rated as attractive, the reward circuit of their brains showed high levels of activation. When the men viewed pictures of women that they rated as average-looking, there was little activation in the reward centers of the brain. At the other end of the spectrum, when the men viewed pictures of attractive males, the reward circuits showed below normal levels of activity—the pleasure system was actually suppressed.

Other studies have shown that the human reward circuit is activated during a wide range of pleasurable behaviors, including laughter and cooperation. In fact, our reward system probably plays a role in almost any behavior that invokes strong feelings. The classic and possibly most stimulating "rewards" to this circuit are food, sex, and drugs (including alcohol and nicotine). All these can be addictive. Thus, it probably comes as no surprise that the reward circuit is thought to be involved in the vicious cycle of addiction. The specific process by which different substances activate the reward circuit varies, as does the force with which the substances produce feelings of pleasure.

The studies of brain activation in the reward circuit during laughter or when looking at pictures of a lover are amusing, but do not convey the critical importance of the reward circuit. As mentioned earlier, the basic function of the reward circuit is to reinforce behaviors that ensure our survival. Additionally, however, it plays an important role in planning a course of action toward a future goal—a strategy at which humans excel, thanks to our exceptionally well-developed prefrontal cortex. Scientists have proposed that the prefrontal cortex acts to modulate the more "primitive" inclinations of other structures in the reward circuit (the VTA and the nucleus accumbens) that are primarily directed toward reward seeking with little regard for possible consequences on future goals. We will talk about how the prefrontal cortex does this in the next chapter.

DOPAMINE—THE REWARD CHEMICAL

Dopamine is a **neurotransmitter**, a chemical that allows neurons to communicate with each other. Dopamine has been implicated as the chemical primarily responsible for activating the reward centers. In early experiments, drug delivery systems were surgically implanted in rats, and the rats were trained to press a lever to initiate drug delivery. In such experiments, the rats learned to give themselves a drug injection any time they pleased.

Initially the drugs that were tested either increased or decreased the levels of known neurotransmitters. Direct injection of neurotransmitters is not always possible. The body has tricks to break down some chemicals quickly so that it does not experience a roller coaster of drug-induced highs and lows. However, scientists learned that an alternate approach worked just as well. They could give drugs that would either increase or decrease the effect of the neurotransmitter in the brain. For example, they could give drugs that would block the ability of neurons to utilize dopamine, causing the brain to feel depleted of dopamine. In other experiments, they might provide a different chemical that would increase dopamine levels. Each time, they would observe the rat's behavior. If the rat pressed the lever often, then it was assumed that the rat liked the feeling produced. If the rat avoided the lever, then it was assumed that it did not like the experience. In fact, this test has been so successful in revealing which substances feel good to rats that it is still widely used in experiments of substance abuse.

It quickly became clear that the rats behaved as if "rewarded" by dopamine. They pressed the lever repeatedly any time a drug

Reward Circuit and Addiction

One of the critical factors leading to substance abuse and addiction is a drug's potent effect on dopamine levels in the brain. For example, heroin increases the neural activity in the dopamine cells, causing them to release more dopamine. Cocaine inhibits the process by which dopamine is cleared from the brain, so that, in the presence of cocaine, dopamine levels rise. Both produce a feeling of intense pleasure and well-being that lasts only as long as the dopamine levels are elevated. When the effect of the drug wears off, the dopamine levels return to normal and the user feels the urge to repeat the experience. Thus, the cycle of addiction begins. Because the adolescent brain is still a work in progress, with fewer tools to modulate the urge for reward acquisition, such as more of an addictive substance, the likelihood that drug or alcohol use will lead to addiction is much higher.

was used that increased the levels of dopamine in its system. Also, if a chemical was used to mimic the neurochemical effects of dopamine, the rats pressed the lever to self-administer the substance over and over again.

Neurons in multiple regions of the brain secrete dopamine, but the most important dopamine pathway for the pleasurable sensation that accompanies reward is the projection from the VTA to the nucleus accumbens. Neurons in the VTA manufacture dopamine. The dopamine is shipped to the nucleus accumbens through the long axonal processes of the VTA neurons. When the VTA neurons are activated (when the brain detects the potential for a reward), they release their dopamine stores into the nucleus accumbens. If the connection between these two structures is disrupted or if the dopamine is blocked, then the experience of a reward is diminished.

More recently, scientists have discovered that some dopamine-secreting cells in the VTA maintain a chronic, low level of activity throughout the day. It is speculated that the consequence of this chronic activity is the steady release of dopamine into the reward circuit. Since dopamine is thought to produce a sense of pleasure or reward, the chronic dopamine release may be important for maintaining mood and preventing excessive mood fluctuations. In fact, some scientists believe that abnormally low levels of dopamine in the reward circuit may contribute to clinical depression. (Other regions of the brain undoubtedly contribute to symptoms of depression, perhaps even to different extents depending on the cause of the depression.)

RISK IS REWARDING

Although it may seem counterintuitive, risk taking and thrill seeking are believed to activate the reward circuit. Remember the sense of sheer dread on Halloween as you and your friends entered the scariest haunted house in your area? You probably have an equally strong memory of the feeling of utter exhilaration when you left the haunted house, having conquered the ghouls and the chainsaw-wielding madman. That exhilaration is compliments of your brain's reward system when it is in high gear.

Each of us has our own threshold for how much thrill we seek and how much risk we can tolerate. For example, when Will needs a rush, he drives fast. Just being in his car makes him feel good. He has it loaded with every gadget on the market that will increase horsepower and improve handling. Just imagining what it would be like to drive a Formula 1 car makes Will's heart race. Yet that is about as much of a thrill as Will wants. He has no urge to climb Mount Everest, and he thinks people who do the daredevil stunts on television are nuts. From a neuroscience perspective, Will has a moderate-to-low threshold for thrills, or, to put it differently, his brain gets a big kick out of relatively mild thrills.

Will's cousin Hoyt is a different matter. Hoyt began riding motocross bikes at the age of 12 (the earliest his parents were willing to let him ride). Over the years as he pushed himself to ride faster and jump higher, Hoyt acquired an impressive variety of injuries. (His mother kept their orthopedic surgeon's phone number on speed dial.) However, the surgeries, casts, and stitches never deterred him from getting back on the motorcycle after he healed. For his eighteenth birthday, the only thing Hoyt wanted was to skydive. He loved it! He now bungee jumps, goes caving, scuba dives, and hopes to do a lot more. He admits that he loves the thrill of being scared out of his mind. Scientists would refer to Hoyt as someone with a high threshold for thrills, a sensation seeker. His brain probably needs a really big thrill to get the same "rush" as Will's brain gets from just driving fast.

Marvin Zuckerman, professor emeritus at the University of Delaware, was the first to speculate that what he called the "sensation seeking" personality trait had a biological basis. He proposed that people have a genetic predisposition to be high, moderate, or low sensation seekers. He also speculated that our genetic makeup dictates how our bodies and brains respond in the face of excitement.

Thus, if Professor Zuckerman's theory is correct, someone like Johnny Knoxville, the co-creator and star of MTV's *Jackass*, probably is genetically predisposed to seek thrills. For Johnny Knoxville, it might seem like a fun idea to ride a grocery cart down a long span of steep stairs. The physiological and biochemical responses of his brain and body might get only moderately charged up by the ride. In contrast, the genetic composition of someone like Will might be very different, at least at the genetic site where the sensation-seeking trait is recorded. Perhaps his brain circuits would signal that the grocery cart ride had more risk than reward, which would make Will resist the ride. If he was forced to do it, his body probably would respond much more powerfully than Johnny Knoxville's, and the experience probably would not be perceived as "fun" by Will. Extremely risk-aversive individuals likely would have severe physical reactions to such an adventure and might experience some of the symptoms of shock, the body's mechanism to deal with extreme stress.

But what does all this have to do with the reward circuit of the brain? Scientists have investigated what happens in brain structures related to reward when animals experience anxiety or risk. A large number of studies have focused on rats, the favorite experimental animal for neuroscientists. Rats tend to be inquisitive and inclined to explore new spaces. In the rat world, safe places are dark and confined. Conversely, open and exposed areas are considered "anxiety-provoking." The scientists speculated that neurotransmitters related to reward might be elevated when rats took risks, such as when they entered the open and exposed spaces.

However, it can be incredibly hard to measure changes in neurotransmitters. Only tiny volumes of neurotransmitter would be released by a brief act such as walking into an open space, and the release may only occur in one specific portion of the brain. To overcome the challenge of detecting tiny neurochemical changes from whole brain samples, scientists devised a tool that allowed them to take localized measurements of neurotransmitters in the brain. This provided information about how neurochemicals were changing locally. In the study of the rats in the anxiety-provoking spaces, scientists looked for changes in dopamine levels because it was known to be related to the reward system. Sure enough, they found that dopamine levels increased when rats ventured into novel spaces. In other experiments, they looked at what would happen if dopamine levels were depleted in the brain. In this case, rats were unwilling to explore the novel space. The conclusion from this series of experiments was that risk-taking triggers dopamine release in the reward circuit, making the experience pleasurable. If no dopamine is present, the behavior is not pleasurable and the rat follows his natural inclination to stay in a more protected environment.

Thanks to MRI technology, it is now possible to look into the human brain and ask how it processes decisions about risk. Dr. Scott Matthews and colleagues from the University of California at San Diego scanned the brains of subjects while they performed a task designed to allow the subjects to earn small monetary awards. The task required subjects to choose between a safe response (where they were guaranteed to win a small monetary award) and a risky response (where there was a chance of winning or losing a larger amount of money). Separately, the test subjects were given a personality test that revealed how strongly an individual was inclined toward behaviors such as novelty seeking, harm avoidance, reward dependence, and persistence.

Individuals who are inclined to be risk takers were expected to choose the risky option more often than the safe option, and individuals characterized to be risk averse were expected to choose the safe option most frequently. The findings showed that one circuit in the brain was activated just before subjects chose the risky option and an entirely different circuit was excited when the subjects chose the safe alternative. Both networks included subdivisions of the prefrontal cortex (as might be expected since this region is involved in decision making) but the nucleus accumbens (a major character in the reward circuit) was activated only when the risky choice was selected. Dr. Matthews and his coworkers concluded from this that indeed risk is rewarding to the brain.

Also when the nucleus accumbens was activated, the amount of activity tended to be stronger in individuals who scored higher on portions of the personality test that predicted a tendency for risk-taking behaviors. The research team interpreted this to mean that the strength of brain activation associated with risky behaviors correlates with an individual's tendency to seek thrills and take risks.

In a similar study, special emphasis was given to the activity in the nucleus accumbens during evaluation of investment strategies. The subjects were required to choose between two stocks and a bond. One stock was randomly designated as a "bad" stock, which was more likely to lose money, and the other was appointed as a "good" stock, which was more likely to make money. The bond promised a safe, low-return payoff. The subjects, who were asked to pick between the two stocks and one bond, did not know which stock was good or bad. They were told if their investment decision had made or lost money, so they could figure out which was the bad stock as the experiment progressed. Yet because it did not lose money on every trial, there remained the temptation to try again and again on the bad stock in hopes of earning more money. Again, the nucleus accumbens was activated when subjects chose the riskier investment, particularly when they decided to invest in the stock whose history had shown it to be potentially bad.

One should not interpret from this that the nucleus accumbens is a region of the brain that makes people do risky things. With more research, it may become apparent that a brain region (or circuit) does have this specific function. However, for now, this research teaches us that behaviors with an element of risk may also have some reward value. Because the brain reinforces behaviors that are rewarding, humans may occasionally take risks, even when other evidence contradicts the impulse. Presumably, if the potential cost of the risk is high (if there is a chance of physical danger, legal ramifications, or big financial loss), the prefrontal cortex will override the tendency of the reward system to seek reward.

RISK AND REWARD IN ADOLESCENTS

Adolescents across the whole of the animal kingdom are much more attracted to novelty than are children or adults (Figure 5.3). Many years ago, Jane Goodall, the legendary anthropologist who studied chimpanzee behavior by living among them and recording details of their daily lives, noted the steady increase in risk-taking behavior as male chimpanzees progress through the adolescent years. Preteen chimps associate almost exclusively with their families. They may associate with chimps outside the immediate family, but only with friends of the family and only if the mother is near. It can be extremely dangerous for young chimps to venture beyond the safety net of the mother because unrelated males (and females to a lesser extent) will attack and on rare occasions even kill vulnerable young chimps.

Once a male chimp reaches adulthood, he will leave the family circle, spending the majority of his time with other males of

Figure 5.3 Teens tend to enjoy risk taking and thrill seeking more than adults do. In this photograph, a teen stimulates her brain by bungee jumping.

his tribe and with breeding females. However, before such independence is achieved, the young male yearns to test his boundaries. During adolescence, he becomes intensely eager to be a part of tribal activities, particularly when there is excitement among the adult males who loudly hoot, beat the ground with their massive hands, and shake bushes and branches to show their ferocity. Despite the intense desire to be involved in the action, the young adolescent dares not join the tribe unless his mother will accompany him. What's more, he will go to considerable lengths to entice her to come with him on his adventure. Dr. Goodall described the adolescents' behavior in this way:

> In response to the excited calling of a party (the adolescent male chimp) may start toward it, then pause and look back at his mother. If she does not follow, he often begins to whimper. He may go farther and stay away for ten minutes or so—but if she still does not come, he usually returns (often still crying).[4]

Female chimps, unlike the males, do not show an urge to get involved in tribal excitement at the early adolescent age. However, once the late adolescent female begins to show signs of sexual maturity, she plunges into the social scene. She will often associate with the adult males of the group and, on occasion, she will leave her tribe and travel to neighboring chimpanzee communities. Typically, this behavior continues until the female chimp delivers her first infant.

Even adolescent rats show an intense urge for novelty and risk taking. In one study, rats were videotaped as they explored a novel space that contained a "safe" (dark and confined) space and an "anxiety-provoking" (open and exposed) space. Adolescent rats (males and females) would first poke their noses into the exposed areas. Quickly thereafter they would extend their bodies into the space in a behavior pattern typical of rats that scientists describe as "risk assessment." After a brief assessment, the adolescents would enter and explore the anxiety-provoking area. The adult rats were every bit as intrigued with the exposed area as were the adolescent rats, and they would spend considerable amounts of time extending their noses and perhaps their torsos into the exposed space, but typically they would not enter the exposed space unless coaxed.

Because of these and many other behavioral studies about the adventurous adolescent period, scientists speculate that increased risk taking might be necessary biologically. After all, the primary job of an adolescent of any species is to develop independence. Thus, if caution and risk aversion ruled the day, adolescents might never get the courage to leave home. To make sure that does not happen, perhaps nature designed adolescents to be attracted to risk, to be willing to explore beyond the safety of family and comfortable surroundings, and to eventually develop the skills needed to survive independently.

But it is not enough to say that adolescents are more adventuresome. In fact, they seem to go about making decisions differently than adults. Multiple studies have compared the decision-making strategies of human adolescents to those used by adults. For example, adolescents tend to favor choices that produce more immediate, as opposed to long-term, outcomes. Adolescents tend to overlook the potential for negative consequence of a decision. Adolescents typically are more motivated by the opportunity for reward than they are deterred by the threat of a negative outcome. Thus, it appears that the adolescent's decision-making machinery operates differently from that of adults.

Experts have proposed a number of explanations for why adolescents make different and often more risky choices than adults. Some have pondered whether there might be disproportional excitatory activity in the reward circuit relative to inhibitory activation, so decisions to engage in risky behaviors do not get suppressed. Others have suggested that perhaps the reward circuit is understimulated, and the adolescents seek more risk to get even a moderate sensation of reward.

Professor James Bjork and colleagues at the National Institute on Alcohol Abuse and Alcoholism looked at patterns of brain activation using the MRI in adolescents and adults. The subjects were trained to recognize cues that represented monetary gains of $0.20, $1.00, or $5.00, or losses of $0.20, $1.00 or $5.00. The task was for the subjects to watch a screen on which the gain/loss cues were projected, wait until they saw a crosshair appear on the screen that indicated that the time for a response was imminent, and then—when the crosshair disappeared—push a button. They had to push the button to get the gain or, alternatively, to avoid the loss. This allowed the scientists to examine brain activity during very precise windows of time when the task was being performed. During the first phase, when the cue was present, the subject was processing the knowledge about possibility for, and relative size of, the gain or loss. When the crosshair was present, the subject was anticipating the opportunity to reap the reward or avoid the loss, and when the crosshair disappeared he or she was performing the required response (pressing the button appropriately). At the end of each sequence, the subjects were told whether they had won or lost money on that trial and were told their cumulative earnings.

The results were very straightforward. In both adults and adolescents, activation patterns in the brain were very similar when the subjects were either making their response, such as pushing the button, and when they were given feedback. Brain activity in both groups also was similar during the phase of the trials when the subjects anticipated the response to avoid losing money. The biggest difference in the comparison between adults and adolescents was in the trials when the subjects anticipated the cue to respond for a monetary gain. The size and amount of activation was significantly more in adults than in adolescents, particularly in the nucleus accumbens (one of the key figures in the reward circuit). Additional areas of the brain were activated during these trials and showed somewhat larger activations in adult brains compared to those of the adolescents, but the difference in the nucleus accumbens was most dramatic.

Bjork and his colleagues speculated that the decreased activity in the nucleus accumbens of adolescents relative to adults was the explanation for the proclivity of adolescents to engage in risky behaviors. Adolescents may need more intense stimulation of their reward centers to compensate for their relatively low levels of activity, according to Bjork's theory. Risks that might produce a sensation of a substantial reward in an adult may have fairly low reward value to an adolescent, so young people seek bigger risks to get the same degree of pleasure.

A subsequent study by Adriana Galvan and coworkers at Cornell University contradicted some of the findings of Bjork's group. Instead, they reported nearly equivalent amounts of activation in the nucleus accumbens of adolescents and adults in response to rewards. However, there were multiple differences in the design of the study compared to that of the Bjork group. For example, Galvan's team collected data on brain activation patterns produced by only the highest rewards. Thus, perhaps adolescents and adults have similar brain-activation patterns when reward values are high, but adolescent brains may be less rewarded when the value of a possible reward is medium or low. In support of the latter alternative, other studies have indicated that young people are less motivated if rewards are modest.

However, Galvan and colleagues garnered important additional information about how the reward circuit functions during adolescence. During the trials they also measured brain activation patterns in the prefrontal cortex. They found that the extent of activation in the prefrontal cortex of adolescents was diffuse and looked more like that of children compared to the focal patterns of activity seen in the prefrontal cortex of adults. Thus, the immature functional capacity of the prefrontal cortex in adolescents likely further contributes to the tendency for adolescents to be risk-takers. Without the oversight and cognitive control of a mature prefrontal cortex, the more impulsive aspects of reward-seeking behaviors (driven in part by the nucleus accumbens) could reign.

■ **Learn more about the contents of this chapter** Search the Internet for *pleasure circuit, risk taking in adolescents,* and *thrill seeking.*

6 | Prefrontal Cortex

Sonya knew that she would be grounded if her room was not cleaned up when her mother got home from work, in a mere 30 minutes or so. Yet she could not resist the urge to check her computer for instant messages to see who was online. When she saw that Otis had signed on, she felt compelled to send him a message.

Otis was incredibly well liked, played starting wide receiver on the football team, and had teased her just yesterday about the doodles she made on her notes in history class. In fact, Sonya had a secrete crush on Otis, and she was delighted when he answered her message. She and Otis chatted online about the upcoming football game, subtly explored what plans each other had for the weekend, and eventually agreed to meet after the game at Jen's party.

Unfortunately, though, Sonya's room was still a mess when her mother got home. Her mother kept her promise and grounded Sonya—through the weekend! Sonya had to learn by text messages about Otis's 26-yard (23.7 meter) catch that set up the only touchdown of the game. It got even worse the following week at school, as everyone—including Otis—told her that Jen's party had been a blast. It probably would not have comforted her at all to have known that her prefrontal cortex had let her down by failing to recognize the long-term benefits of cleaning her room on time.

As noted earlier, the prefrontal cortex is one of the last regions of the cerebral cortex to develop in the adolescent brain; in fact, the final growth surge and refinement of the prefrontal cortex does not occur until early adulthood. The prefrontal cortex has been referred to as the CEO (chief executive officer) of the brain and acts as the contemplative, rational supervisor of the other parts of the brain. So if the prefrontal cortex is not yet developed in teens, other parts of the brain can dominate behavior. Enter the emotional brain, called the **limbic system**, which is working at full speed in adolescents. Scientists speculate that the limbic system may play a dominant role in the adolescent thought process, which could explain why adolescents have a difficult time suppressing emotional and impulsive behaviors. In this chapter, we will get to know more about the prefrontal cortex and its function in the adult brain. Then we will discuss research evidence indicating that the prefrontal cortex does not function in adolescents the way it does in adults.

PREFRONTAL CORTEX IN ADULTS

You use your prefrontal cortex (Figure 6.1) to help you set priorities (such as planning which school assignment to tackle first), and also as you work toward long-range goals (such as attending college). If it is working as it should, your prefrontal cortex will help you ignore distractions that will keep you from finishing the work. Your prefrontal cortex helps you use all the social skills at your disposal in social situations. How it does all this is not fully known, but research about the prefrontal cortex is well under way.

As noted earlier, the prefrontal cortex is integrally involved in making decisions about the potential for reward and possible consequences of risk. Most of our understanding of its role in the reward circuit comes from studies in our close relatives, monkeys. Ultrafine recording electrodes can be permanently

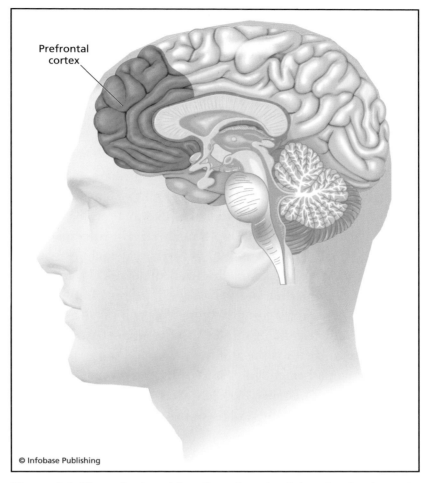

Prefrontal
cortex

© Infobase Publishing

Figure 6.1 The extent and location of prefrontal cortex is shown in red. The prefrontal cortex is referred to as the chief executive officer of the brain because of its critical involvement in planning and decision making.

inserted into the brain of a monkey so that the activity of neurons can be monitored as the monkey performs specific tasks. Recordings from the prefrontal cortex indicate that some prefrontal neurons are activated when a reward is received, others respond if a reward is anticipated but not received, and yet other neurons signal if the expected reward will be large versus small, and if it will be highly pleasurable (such as a yummy treat) versus merely palatable (such as a serving of the daily meal). The neurons even signal to show preference for specific rewards. For example, a neuron might respond in favor of reward B if the monkey is shown rewards A and B, but the same cell might respond in favor of reward C if the monkey is shown rewards B and C.

The prefrontal cortex gets a tremendous amount of information from nearly all other higher-order brain systems. Therefore, even when tempted with the lure of a potential reward, the prefrontal cortex processes all additional, relevant information at hand before making a decision. Decisions may include whether to plan a strategy to obtain the immediate reward, to forego the present temptation and persist with the ongoing behavior, or perhaps to adapt a completely new behavioral strategy with yet a different reward in mind. Another important feature of the prefrontal cortex is the ability to maintain the goal-directed behavior over an extended period of time. This may be critical for our ability to choose between a reward that is immediate but has relatively minor reward value, versus a delayed reward of considerably greater value. Thus, thanks to the prefrontal cortex, a high school sophomore might have enough foresight to turn down an invitation to a movie the night before the math final in favor of getting a good grade in math with the ultimate goal of being accepted into a highly ranked engineering school.

Another important feature of the prefrontal cortex is its role in **working memory**. Working memory is the ability to hold information "online" while performing an unrelated task, then retrieving the memory later. For example, imagine that you are waiting for a call from your best friend to tell you when to meet at the movie theater. The phone rings and it is your mother, asking you to pick up a few groceries after the movie. While you are still talking to your mom, you hear the phone beeping to tell you that someone else is trying to call. You promise to get the groceries that your mom requested, tell her good-bye, and pick up the new call. Later, after you have made plans to meet for the movie, you write down the list of groceries that your mom asked you to pick up.

The ability to remember the list of groceries while making plans for the movie is working memory. Patricia Goldman-Rakic was a professor at Yale University for many years and became world famous for her work on the role of the prefrontal cortex in working memory. Working memory may be one of the most critical components of higher brain function for goal-directed behaviors. A fairly simple example of a goal-directed behavior is whatever behavior is required to achieve a specific goal, even a goal that is delayed in time. Goal-directed behaviors are important for our ability to choose between a reward that is immediate but has relatively minor reward value versus a delayed reward of greater value. This capacity to wait for a reward is a hallmark of the human adult brain. In some cases, the prefrontal cortex may be required to make adjustments to behavioral strategies and possibly even long-term goals if conditions, such as rewards or risks, shift over time.

In most animals, the prefrontal cortex is rather small. In nonhuman primates, such as monkeys, chimps, and gorillas, the prefrontal cortex is large relative to that of other nonprimate species. However, this region reaches its maximum size in humans (Figure 6.2). One benefit of this enormous brain expansion is the capacity to plan and execute a strategy to obtain long-term goals.

Even a task as mundane as executing a strategy to get all course requirements needed for college is a sophisticated feat for the brain. It requires us to first select a strategy for completing all the coursework on time, then to perform behaviors that

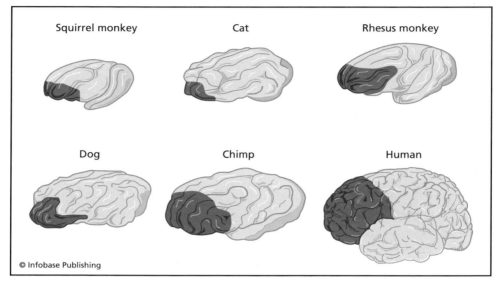

Figure 6.2 The relative size of the prefrontal cortex across a range of species is depicted in this illustration. The prefrontal cortex of humans takes up a larger percentage of their brain than any other species.

ensure the attainment of each step in the strategy, and finally to continue to make adjustments to the strategy to maximize your options. For example, perhaps the college preparation plan that you start out with includes only the minimum number of math classes necessary to get into the nearby junior college. You complete Math I and Math II in your freshman and sophomore years, and you make good grades in both classes. In fact, you have made mostly A's and B's in all your classes. The college counselor thinks that you might be able to get a scholarship to a major university if you keep your grades up. However, the big universities often prefer that students take 4 years of math class during high school, so you adjust your college plan and add an additional math class.

The prefrontal cortex processes the enormous range of information needed for planning and decision making. Functions of the prefrontal cortex include the capacity to weigh good and bad options and make appropriate decisions, to evaluate possible consequences (potential rewards as well as risks) based on existing information, and to suppress socially unacceptable or excessively emotional behaviors.

There are many behaviors that represent unconscious responses to our environment that do not require our attention or demand that we make choices. These spontaneous behaviors are wired into our nervous systems, either genetically or by virtue of many repetitions of practice. For example, throwing a ball with incredible accuracy becomes natural if it is practiced enough. However, baseball players typically cannot tell you every little adjustment that they make in preparation to throw a ball. They just go through the process without thinking much about it. Highly familiar behaviors such as baseball throwing become imprinted on our brains so the process happens almost without thought. From a scientific perspective, these behaviors rely on neural circuits that have become entrenched in the brain. The circuits execute the appropriate sequence of motor behaviors without conscious thought.

However, imagine that you are playing catch in the yard while neighborhood children of all ages scamper about, including your little sister, whom you have been instructed to watch. Winding up to throw the ball, you hear the long squeal of car tires in a hard brake and the extended honk of a car horn. You quickly comprehend that the sounds could signal danger, perhaps to your sister or one of the younger children who may have wandered into the road and into harm's way. You stop the action of throwing the ball and turn toward the road. In the same fraction of a second you mentally locate a parent or another adult in charge so that you can seek help if necessary. In that same brief time you realize that the squealing tires came from a car that ran the stop sign. It nearly hit a car that had the right of way, and whose driver was angrily blasting his horn. You see that your sister is safe; she is still on the porch playing with the neighbor's puppy. You resume the game of catch. Although this complex sequence of behaviors took place over the course of only a second or two, it required a fairly sophisticated measure of control and conscious decision. That was the prefrontal cortex at work.

Some authors have dubbed the prefrontal cortex the "etiquette police" because it counterbalances the impulsive tendencies of the emotional part of the brain. The region of the brain known for its role in emotion is called the limbic system. The limbic system is a group of structures that has a number of functions in addition to processing emotion, including motivation, impulsiveness, and memory. The limbic system has control over behaviors that include unconscious reactions to fear-provoking stimuli and it mediates the famous fight-or-flight response.

Imagine that you and your friends are at the mall when you encounter the school principal. Because you have been in her office two times already this year, she knows you well. The principal stops to say hello but has a suspicious expression on her face, as though she assumes you and your friends are getting into trouble. Her tendency to expect that kids are up to mischief makes you furious. However, if it is working properly, your prefrontal cortex squashes your inclination to blurt out a sarcastic remark.

The whole spectrum of functions performed by the prefrontal cortex leads to the conclusion that the prefrontal cortex provides a supervisory function over the more impulsive tendencies. Some of the earliest evidence for this came from the famous patient Phineas Gage, who suffered a massive injury to his prefrontal cortex more than a century ago (Figure 6.3). Gage was working as a foreman on a railroad

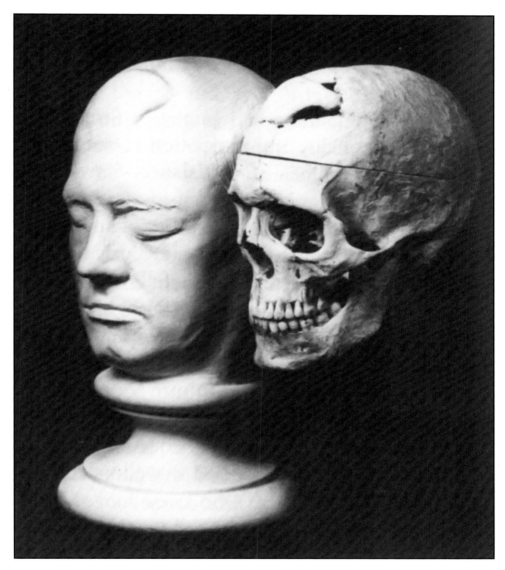

Figure 6.3 A death mask of Phineas Gage is seen beside his skull, which had been fractured by an iron rod. Despite the massive injury to his prefrontal cortex, Gage lived for another 12 years. Many believed, however, that his personality was radically changed by the accident.

construction crew when an explosive charge went off pre-maturely. The blast drove the tamping iron that Gage was using upward, through his head. A tamping iron is a long, tapered rod shaped like the javelin that is used in track and field events. According to Malcolm MacMillan at Deakin University in Victoria, Australia, who is an expert on the story of Phineas Gage, the rod was more than 3 feet long (1 m), over an inch (2.5 centimeters) in diameter and weighed more than 13 pounds (5.9 kilograms). The point of the iron went in through Gage's left cheek, shattered his upper jaw, coursed behind his left eye and through the left side of his frontal lobe and finally exited out the top of his head on the left side. Gage fell over after being struck but news reports indicated that he never lost consciousness.

As one might expect, given that Gage suffered considerable damage to his face and left frontal lobe, it was many weeks before he had recovered well enough to return to work. But his personality had changed so much as a result of the injury that he was not able to maintain his role as crew foreman. Notes made by Gage's treating physician described the effects of the injury on Gage's personality this way:

> Before the accident (Gage) had been their most capa-ble and efficient foreman, one with a well-balanced mind, and who was looked on as a shrewd smart busi-ness man. He was now fitful, irreverent, and grossly profane, showing little deference for his fellows. He was also impatient and obstinate, yet capricious and vacillating, unable to settle on any of the plans he devised for future action. His friends said he was "No longer Gage."[5]

The story of Phineas Gage is a particularly extreme example of traumatic injury to the prefrontal cortex but a number of studies since then have confirmed that prefrontal cortex injury leads to disruption of personality and motivation.

Recently, Daria Knoch of University Hospital of Zurich and colleagues designed an ingenious study to disable the prefrontal cortex briefly and evaluate the impact on behavior. They applied mild magnetic stimulation to either the left or right forehead of the subjects for 15 minutes. Then the subjects were asked to perform a gambling paradigm designed to measure willingness to take risks in decision making. The magnetic stimulation briefly disrupted local brain activity, and the placement of the stimulator was selected to disrupt the activity of either the right or left prefrontal cortex. Without stimulation, or after a "sham" stimulation when the experimenters pretended to pass magnetic current, the subjects showed the normal tendencies toward optimizing chances for reward and minimizing risk. However, after magnetic disruption of brain activity in the right frontal cortex, subjects were more likely to choose the high-risk option, and they earned significantly fewer points in the gambling paradigm. The researchers speculated that the right prefrontal cortex normally provides control over behaviors that are impulsive or risky.

PREFRONTAL CORTEX IN ADOLESCENTS

After the discovery was made that the prefrontal cortex is one of the last parts of the brain to mature, researchers began to wonder if the emotional excesses and impulsiveness of adolescents could reflect the lack of an "override" by a mature prefrontal cortex. We have already seen from the previous chapter that teen brains show almost childlike patterns of activity in the prefrontal cortex when performing a task that involves a chance of monetary gain (reward) or loss (risk). The investigators of that study concluded that a mature prefrontal cortex is needed to provide overseeing and cognitive control over impulsive, reward-seeking behaviors. To make matters worse, the impulsive urge to seek rewards is nearly fully developed in adolescents.

One particularly critical function of the prefrontal cortex is attention. The ability to focus our attention is crucial because

Schizophrenia, the Prefrontal Cortex, and Dopamine

Research findings suggest that malfunctions in the prefrontal cortex may contribute to schizophrenia, a neurological disease that leads to disrupted thought processes, distortions of reality, violent emotional swings, and difficulties with memory and attention. Symptoms of schizophrenia often first emerge in adolescence. Noninvasive imaging studies of individuals who have been diagnosed with schizophrenia show disrupted function in some areas of the prefrontal cortex. Also, autopsy studies of schizophrenic brains have revealed abnormalities in the prefrontal cortex.

As shown in the illustration to the right, neurons in prefrontal cortex are targeted by inputs that contain high concentrations of the neurotransmitter dopamine. The dopamine-rich inputs make synaptic contact with the dendrites of the prefrontal neurons (see magnified image in the adjacent picture). Disruptions of synaptic transmission at this dopamine synapse likely contribute to some symptoms of schizophrenia.

Most anti-psychotic drugs that are used to treat symptoms of schizophrenia block dopamine receptors. Because of this, researchers have proposed that the psychotic state that accompanies schizophrenia may be due to an overactive dopamine system. Unfortunately, current medications do not completely cure the disease, but simply relieve symptoms.

our brains are constantly being bombarded with stimuli. Even when virtually nothing is going on in our external world, our brain is busy in ways that we never imagine. Here are a few examples: Our joints send information to the brain to help

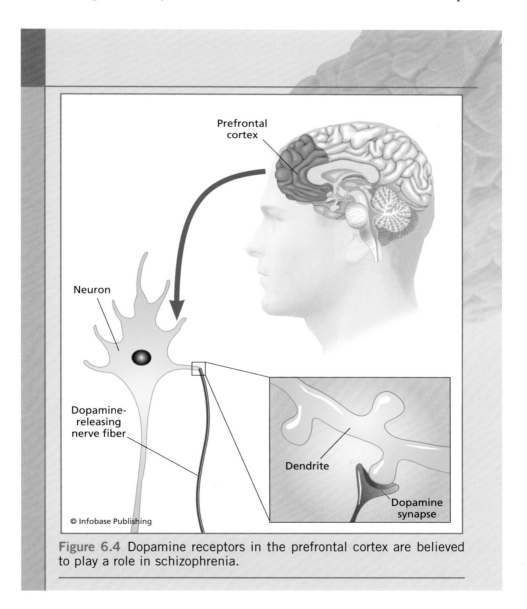

Figure 6.4 Dopamine receptors in the prefrontal cortex are believed to play a role in schizophrenia.

maintain posture; our eyes, ears, mouth, and nose relay input to the brain about background levels of sensory activity; and our cerebellum is firing away, keeping our movements natural and thought-free—all without our notice. In order to direct our attention, our brain must be able to tune out all this background activity and focus on the information that is important. Although we do not understand how it is done, the prefrontal cortex is involved in directing our attention.

Christopher Monk and his colleagues from the National Institute of Mental Health devised an imaginative experiment to compare activity in the prefrontal cortex of adults with that of adolescents while they were doing a task that required mental focus and attention. They asked the subjects to direct their attention to specific features of a face in a photo. The trick was that the face was posed in a variety of intensely emotional expressions (such as fear, anger, or happiness).

A face is a critically important visual stimulus to a human. Recognition of faces and interpretation of facial expressions are essential for human interactions. Studies in newborn human infants indicate that a face is strongly preferred among other visual stimuli. A highly emotional face is even more compelling, perhaps for survival reasons. The ability to recognize and avoid someone in a rage or intent on causing harm probably was an essential survival skill for early human ancestors and remains an important skill today. Expressions such as anger and fear strongly activate the emotional centers in the limbic system.

Monk and his group used MRI to measure the activity in the prefrontal cortex and other regions of the brain involved in emotion, including the limbic system, while the subjects were viewing the pictures of faces. The critical test was the measure of brain activity during a period when the subjects were asked to focus on a specific facial feature (such as nose width). Compared to adolescents, adults had higher activity in the prefrontal cortex when performing the attention task. Adolescent brains showed robust activity in the prefrontal cortex, but not when required to perform the attention task. The investigators interpreted the results as suggesting that adolescents are poor at maintaining attention when presented with emotionally compelling distractions.

Other laboratories are also looking for maturational changes in the prefrontal cortex during the adolescent period. Presumably, behaviors mediated by the prefrontal cortex (working memory, decision making, and reward/risk assessment) are not adultlike until the structural and functional development of the prefrontal cortex is complete. Although there are differences in research results, the general conclusion is that the functional capacity of the prefrontal cortex in adolescents is limited.

To complicate matters, the more emotional parts of the brain may be in hyperdrive. For example, in an MRI study of the activity in the temporal lobe (a part of the limbic system), Vinod Menon and colleagues at Stanford University found that between the ages of 10 and 20 years, temporal lobe activity dramatically decreases. Brain activity was measured while subjects performed a task that the investigators referred to as memory encoding. It should be stressed that the activity did not reflect emotion or impulsivity, or any of the other traits that are common in adolescents. However, the overall finding of high levels of activity in this part of the temporal lobe in children and young teens, followed by dramatic decreases by 20 years of age, lends strength to the argument that the emotional brain may hijack the thinking brain (prefrontal cortex) during adolescence.

■ **Learn more about the contents of this chapter**   Search the Internet for *working memory*, *Phineas Gage*, and *facial recognition*.

7 | Hormones and the Brain

Jillian bounced into the kitchen soon after her mom announced dinner and greeted everyone with an animated air. Even her older brother and current archenemy, Jason, was granted a smile. Jillian's cheerfulness seemed to permeate the whole room and everyone sat down to the meal in high spirits. Jillian's dad was especially pleased. As his only daughter, Jillian held a special place in his heart. She used to refer to herself as "daddy's girl."

During the meal, conversation was exceptionally light-hearted. Jillian kept everyone entertained with wildly exaggerated accounts of the newest drama in her ninth-grade class. Jillian's three brothers were infected with the silliness and tried to outdo Jillian with their own stories of teenage exploits. Then the mood began to shift. Jason challenged Jillian's remark that females are the superior sex. The other brothers quickly leapt to the defense of men, and Jillian found herself arguing against all three boys. The last straw was when her dad took exception to her comment that all men are immature. Jillian erupted into a rage. Worst of all, she turned her venom on her dad, who she felt had betrayed her because he sided with her brothers. She screamed, "I hate you!" and stormed out of the kitchen and up to her room. Later that same night, Jillian could not even recall what had made her so furious.

The teenage years are characterized as a roller coaster of emotional highs and lows often coming in rapid succession, as was the case with Jillian. Scientists believe that the emotional surges may reflect the impact of the puberty hormones, estrogen and testosterone, on brain function. As we will discuss in this chapter, the puberty hormones target receptors in multiple regions of the brain, including areas known to be involved in the processing of emotion. In fact, a wide spectrum of behavioral disruptions that accompany puberty could result from the impact of hormones on the brain.

EFFECTS OF THE PUBERTY HORMONES

Only your brain knows when your body is scheduled to begin puberty. When that time arrives, a hormone called **gonadotropin-releasing hormone** (GnRH) is released from a region at the very base of the brain, called the **hypothalamus**, which controls many of our primitive life functions (such as temperature regulation, hunger and thirst, circadian cycles). GnRH travels through the bloodstream to the nearby **pituitary gland** (Figure 7.1) and signals cells in the anterior (front) part of the pituitary gland to begin producing two other puberty hormones, **luteinizing hormone** (LH) and **follicle-stimulating hormone** (FSH). In boys and girls, the process is identical up to this point, but the different effects of LH and FSH on males and females are what make boys into men and girls into women.

In boys, the LH and FSH hormones leave the pituitary gland and travel through the bloodstream to the genitals, where they signal the testes to begin the production of testosterone, the principal male sex hormone. Testosterone is released into the bloodstream and carried throughout the body to a wide variety of target tissues. In the tissues, testosterone can activate two types of receptors. The **androgen receptor** is typically associated with testosterone and the expression of male features. In addition, testosterone is converted to **estradiol** (one of several forms

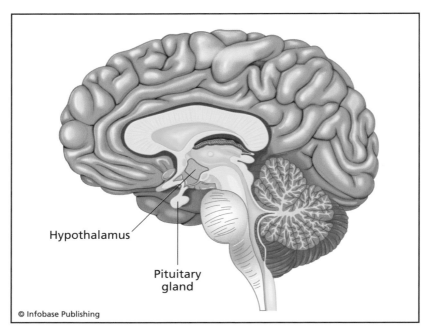

© Infobase Publishing

Figure 7.1 The location of the hypothalamus and the pituitary gland are shown in this cross-section of a human brain. The signal for puberty to begin is a hormone, released by neurons in the hypothalamus, that targets the pituitary gland.

of estrogen) that activates some **estrogen receptors** (typically associated with female characteristics). However, the estradiol in males does not initiate the expression of female physical characteristics. In fact, both males and females produce "male" and "female" hormones, but the proportions differ. Adult males produce about 20 times more testosterone than females. Therefore, the physical expression of male traits dominates.

The action of the testosterone on the testosterone receptors in the various tissues of the body is what initiates the physical changes that accompany puberty in males. The male genitalia develop and begin to produce viable semen, the notorious teenage growth spurt is triggered, coarse hair emerges, the vocal cords lengthen, pimples become a frequent nuisance, and body odor intensifies. Relatively little attention is given to the fact that testosterone receptors also are present in the brain. So when puberty hits and testosterone surges, the brain is affected just as profoundly as the rest of the body. Specific details about the impact of puberty hormones on the brain are discussed below.

In girls, the FSH and LH that is released from the pituitary glands at puberty travel through the bloodstream to the ovaries, the female equivalent of the male testes. The hormones stimulate the ovaries to begin producing hormones called estrogen and progesterone. A number of cells in the body produce these hormones, but the ovaries produce the highest concentrations in females of reproductive age. Testosterone also is produced by some cells in females but the concentrations are much lower than in males.

Estrogen is produced in multiple forms. The principle form of estrogen, estradiol, is produced primarily by the ovaries. Estrogens are also produced in smaller amounts by other tissues, including those in the breasts. Estrogen activates two types of receptors, the alpha (ERα) and beta (ERβ) estrogen receptors. ERα receptors are found in the uterus, ovaries, and the hypothalamus. ERβ receptors are located in nonreproductive tissues, including the brain.

The action of the estrogen on the estrogen receptors in the various tissues of the body is what initiates the physical changes that accompany puberty in females. The breasts develop, the hips widen, the percentage of body fat increases, and menstruation begins. Other physical changes that are triggered at puberty are the same in girls as in boys, including coarse hair under the arms and in the pubic area, pimples, and body odor. Estrogen also acts on receptors that are widely distributed throughout the brain, the ERβ receptors.

Progesterone plays little or no role in the expression of puberty. Progesterone has a complex role in pregnancy and lactation, but its functions are outside the scope of this book.

IMPACT OF PUBERTY HORMONES ON THE BRAIN

The brain has widespread sex hormone (testosterone and estrogen) receptors. This means that when puberty hits, it acts on the brain just as powerfully as it does the body. Many of the sex hormone receptors are concentrated in the hypothalamus, which plays an important role in sexual behavior. The hypothalamus is composed of multiple neuronal groupings that have specific functions in regulating primitive body functions. For example, based on research in rats, we know that the medial preoptic region of the hypothalamus controls male sexual behaviors such as erection, mounting, and ejaculation. The ventral regions of the hypothalamus control female sexual behaviors, such as a posturing reflex called lordosis. Although the specific role of the preoptic area in humans is unknown, it is approximately two times larger in males than in females, and so it is assumed to play a role in gender-specific behavior or function.

Initially, evidence of sex hormone receptors throughout the brain puzzled scientists. Scientists assumed that these hormones only played a role in sexual function and wondered why the brain would produce receptors for sex hormones in regions that had nothing to do with reproduction and related behaviors. However, now the presence of both testosterone and estrogen receptors in diverse regions of the brain is well established. We still do not understand the role of the sex hormones on these various brain regions, but we assume that they play a role in behavior. The second point is that when these hormones flood the circulatory system at puberty, their effects on the brain undoubtedly are profound.

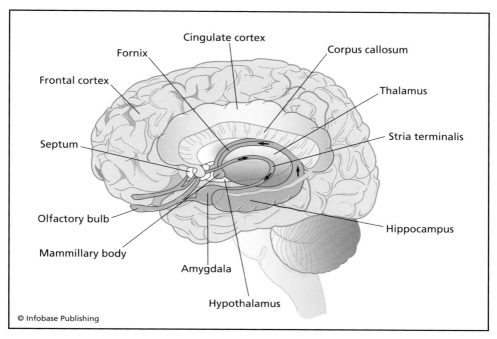

Figure 7.2 Shown in this drawing are the structures of the limbic system. The stria terminalis is a major nerve fiber highway that carries information to and from the amygdala. The fornix is a major nerve fiber highway of the hippocampus. Physiologist Paul MacLean gave the limbic system its name because it forms a limbus, or ring, around the thalamus.

The amygdala is one of the brain regions where puberty hormones are found. The amygdala is located in the temporal lobes and is considered to be part of the limbic system, part of the brain that controls emotion (Figure 7.2). Early research suggested that the amygdala was involved chiefly in the expression of fear and rage. Electrical stimulation of one region of the amygdala elicited an "arrest" reaction, in which the animal froze and assumed an attitude of attention, as if preparing for flight or fight. Stimulation of another part of the amygdala triggered rage. The animals hissed, growled, and showed classic emotion-related autonomic responses, including increased respiration and dilated pupils. Another part of the amygdala is involved with the sense of smell (**olfaction**) and olfactory-related functions such as pheromone processing.

More recent research suggests that yet another part of the amygdala is involved with the formation of memories that have an emotional component. For example, after eating lunch in the high school cafeteria every day during freshman and sophomore years, Jake has little memory of what he ate. Lunches all seem to merge together into a big blur. However, Jake can remember every detail about the lunch that was served the day that a football landed in the middle of his plate. He was a lowly freshman at that time and avoided the upper class boys as much as he could because they loved to taunt freshmen. Apparently a football had been thrown by the starting quarterback to one of his lineman (who obviously could not catch). It was tipped in the air and landed in Jake's food. The whole room erupted with laughter, especially the football boys. Jake laughed as loudly as everyone else, pretending that he thought it was funny. He wiped the food off of the ball and sent it sailing back to the quarterback. But being the target of everyone's laughter was deeply embarrassing to Jake. The emotional surge that accompanied the event seared the memory of every detail of that lunch in Jake's brain.

Jake's amygdala was responsible for the intensity of that memory. As part of the limbic system, the amygdala contributes to the formation of long-term memories, particularly memories with an emotional component. If a memory is formed when the amygdala is highly activated (by strong emotion), the vividness and durability of the memory are reinforced.

Receptors for the puberty hormones have also been found in the hippocampus. As part of the limbic system, the hippocampus is critical for the formation of long-term memories. Damage to the hippocampus usually results in an inability to form new memories. A special feature of the hippocampus is its role in navigation, also called spatial memory. Damage to a part of the hippocampus interferes with a person's ability to remember the places where he or she has been and how to find a route from one place to another.

The cerebellum is another major brain structure found to have receptors for the puberty hormones. The cerebellum is located at the back of the head just above the junction between the head and neck. It is a complex structure with many subdivisions. Historically, the cerebellum has been associated with the motor system, especially in the coordination and fine-tuning of movements. The cerebellum also integrates sensory and motor information to stabilize posture and maintain balance. Recent studies suggest that the cerebellum may be involved in a wide range of complex brain functions including attention, memory, and language.

The presence of puberty hormone receptors in all the structures described above indicates that the function of these structures might be altered by the high concentrations of testosterone (in boys) and estrogen (in girls) that are released at puberty. For example, because the amygdala is involved in emotion, perhaps the presence of the puberty hormones in the adolescent amygdala contributes to the emotional upheavals that punctuate the teenage years. Also, perhaps puberty hormones influence memory formation in the hippocampus. If this is the case, then parents should be encouraged to give their teens a little extra consideration, rather than threats of punishment, if they only remember the first of a list of chores assigned to them. Finally, maybe the gangly arms and legs aren't the only culprits for the lack of coordination typical of the teenage years. Instead, the appearance of puberty hormones in the cerebellum of adolescents may alter the ability to integrate sensory information and generate smoothly coordinated movements.

SEXUALITY AND THE BRAIN

Scientists believe that the sexual identity of the brain is determined by the hormonal mixture present early in development. Early exposure to sex hormones has permanent effects on brain organization. Scientists suggest that, very early in development, the brains of both sexes are similar or perhaps even identical. Then, for a short period, the testes in fetal males produce testosterone (and then go dormant until puberty). Scientists believe that this brief pulse of testosterone, very early in the development of males, instructs the brain to become "male." If testosterone is not present during this window of fetal development, then the brain stays "female."

Most evidence for this comes from rats, the favorite animal model for research on hormonal influences. Rats are born with extremely underdeveloped brains so procedures performed after birth in a rat are comparable to events that occur *in utero* in humans. This allows scientists to determine how external factors (such as hormones) impact brain development.

There is an area near the hypothalamus called the **sexually dimorphic nucleus of the preoptic area** (SDN-POA) that is five to six times larger in male rats than in females (Figure 7.3). If a female rat is injected with testosterone just after birth, her brain develops a significantly larger SDN-POA. Conversely, elimination of testosterone in neonatal males causes a decrease in the size of the SDN-POA. These findings support the idea that the brain is instructed to become male by the presence of testosterone early in life or allowed to remain female in the absence of testosterone.

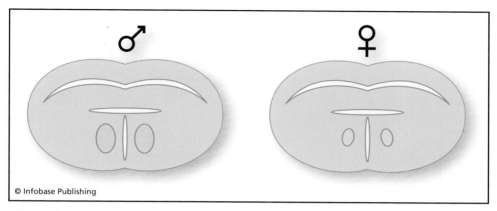

© Infobase Publishing

Figure 7.3 The sexually dimorphic nucleus of the preoptic area of males (blue) is much larger than in females (pink), as seen in the illustrated cross-section of the hypothalamus above.

A human condition (called testicular feminizing syndrome) provides confirmation of this theory. Testicular feminizing syndrome affects genetic males and causes a lack of responsiveness to testosterone during fetal life. Males born with this condition develop female-like genitalia and have female-like sexual preferences.

Even though the brain is assigned a sex early in development, scientists believe that the expression of gender-specific sexual behaviors does not emerge until puberty. During this stage of development, exposure to high levels of sexual hormones triggers male- and female-specific behaviors. Most of the evidence for this hypothesis comes from studies in rats. If rats are surgically sterilized before puberty, they do not show gender-specific behaviors such as sexual posturing (body positions unique to either male or female rodents that are thought to indicate sexual receptiveness). Then, if given doses of the appropriate hormone (testosterone for male rats or estrogen for females), the rats promptly assume all the gender-typical sexual behaviors. In humans, the expression of gender-specific behaviors is much more complex and probably regulated by a multitude of influences. However, many scientists believe that, even in humans, the brain is masculinized if testosterone is present early in fetal development. Then at puberty, the re-expression of testosterone will produce behaviors typical of males (e.g., aggressiveness). Conversely, in the absence of testosterone early in fetal development, the brain retains its default organization, which some scientists refer to as the feminine brain.

■ **Learn more about the contents of this chapter** Search the Internet for *pituitary gland*, *limbic system*, and *sex hormones*.

8 | Adolescent Sleep Cycles

As a girl, Kayla had no trouble going to bed. In fact, she usually welcomed the nightly bedtime readings and quiet talk with her mom. On most nights, if she was not already asleep by 9:00 P.M., she was at least well on her way. Better yet, Kayla slept well most nights and greeted each new day with a smile, even at 6:30 on school mornings when her mother woke her. But soon after Kayla started junior high, she began to resent bedtime. Kayla felt that she was too old for the bedtime stories that her mom still told, particularly because her older brother, Jalen, called them "baby stories." When Jalen started ninth grade, he was allowed to stay up later than Kayla and it made her fume to see him watching television while she was being herded off to her bedroom. The worst part of it all was that she just was not sleepy and would lie in bed with her mind churning for what seemed like hours.

By the time Kayla started ninth grade, she had developed a wide assortment of activities to entertain herself after she went into her bedroom for the night. She did not even care that her mom allowed her to stay up as late as Jalen because there was plenty to do in her room. Kayla would listen to music, using headphones after she was reminded to go to sleep so her mom would not hear the music. She would bury her head under the covers and talk on the phone to her friends. Kayla even took up poetry writing for awhile and often lost all track of time as she worked. Typically, she did not mean to stay up as late as she did, but time just seemed to get away from her.

By the time that Kayla was a junior in high school, she was exhausted all the time. She would sleep from the time she got home from school until dinner. She would do her schoolwork until bedtime and then spend the next few hours catching up with friends by phone or instant messaging. On school mornings, she could hardly get out of bed. She was frequently tearful and usually grumpy, and her grades had shown a dramatic decline. Her mother became so concerned that she took Kayla to see a doctor who ran all sorts of test to rule out horrible-sounding things such as anemia, thyroid problems, and even leukemia. All tests came back normal, which reassured Kayla's mom. However, Kayla continued to worry, because it was so hard for her to stay awake during the day.

Everything changed when Kayla's mom saw her final grades for the first semester of her junior year. They were bad, even in Kayla's opinion. Kayla's mom was so mad that Kayla was practically under house arrest. Her mom even supervised her while she did her homework and would not let her have the television or phone in her room at night.

But a strange thing happened. Without all the nighttime distractions, Kayla discovered that it was easier to quiet her thoughts, and she actually began to fall asleep at about 11:00 P.M. (what her mother called a "decent time") rather than at 1:00 or 2:00 in the morning. Kayla still felt like a grump in the morning, but she could at least stay awake in class. She was not nearly as sleepy after school, so she did her homework instead of taking an afternoon nap. In the absence of a nap, Kayla actually welcomed bedtime and fell asleep promptly once the lights were off. She even began to feel less emotional and, as a result, managed to make peace with her mom. Best of all, Kayla's grades improved. Kayla eventually regained all the privileges that her mom had taken away.

It is not at all unusual for teens to experience chronic sleepiness. Unfortunately, because of the ever-increasing number of electronics in the bedrooms of teens in the United States, cases like Kayla's are becoming more common. One study found that, by the time teens are high school seniors, they have an average of four electronic gadgets in their room to provide nighttime distraction.

However, scientists have found new evidence that suggests that the primary culprit for sleeplessness in teens is a region of the brain that dictates our sleep/wake cycles. For reasons that still are unclear, sleep/wake cycles get shifted during adolescence. As a result, it is harder for teens to fall asleep at a moderate hour at night, and it is nearly impossible for them to wake up in the morning—particularly at the early hours dictated by most school systems.

Before we talk about the details of the new findings on sleep disturbances in adolescents, let's review the biology of sleep and consider why sleep is so important.

WHAT IS SLEEP?

Some animals spend more than 80% of the day asleep. The human infant sleeps for about 60% of the day. Nearly a third of an adult's life is devoted to sleep. During sleep, body movements are reduced and there is a decreased awareness of surroundings. Unlike a coma or hibernation, sleep is easily interrupted by external stimulation, such as light or a loud noise.

Why is sleep so important? Truth be told, the purpose of sleep is still a mystery. Although sleep seems to be a restful time, the brain is progressing through stages of sleep cycles. During the first period of sleep, measurements taken with a machine that measures brain waves, called an **electroencephalograph,** show that brain waves slow down. Over the course of the first hour or so, the brain settles into progressively deeper stages of slow-wave sleep. If people are awakened during this phase, they remember only fragments of thoughts, not dreams. Subsequently, the brain reverses itself and progresses back through the earlier stages of slow-wave sleep, and it enters a period of high brain activity that mirrors wakefulness. The eyes may move back and forth, making rapid eye movements (REMs) and if people are awakened during this phase, they often report vivid dreaming. During the remainder of the night the brain alternates through these two extremes of deep slow-wave sleep and REM sleep, with more and more time spent in REM sleep (Figure 8.1).

Sleep has several functions. The most obvious reason for sleep is to offer a pause in physical activity. When we sleep we conserve energy, and long periods of sleep reduce the amount of energy we are required to consume in the form of food. Animals that have very high metabolisms typically require the most sleep in a 24-hour period. In addition, a wide assortment of other body and brain process seems to benefit from sleep.

Most of what we know about the effects of sleep comes from sleep deprivation studies in which an experimental animal (usually a rat) or human is startled or stimulated whenever it begins to fall asleep. Extreme sleep deprivation can be fatal. This evidence comes from studies in rats that were sleep deprived for several weeks. Over time, the rats lost weight (even though they were eating more than usual). They lost the ability to regulate their body temperature and acted like they could not get warm enough. Also the rats developed severe systemic infections that were described as the ultimate cause of death.

Most studies of the effects of sleep deprivation are not nearly so severe. But even short periods of sleep deprivation have consequences. For example, the brain's energy stores become

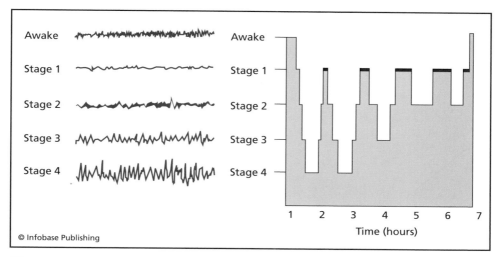

Figure 8.1 Examples of brain wave patterns measured by electroencephalography (EEG) are shown in red. During the initial phase of sleep (Stage 1), brain waves slow down, but as sleep progresses the brain wave activity increases (Stages 2–4). The most active phase of sleep, rapid eye movement (REM) sleep, is similar to wakefulness. The plot at right shows that brain wave activity alternates over the course of a night between light and deep sleep with progressively longer times spent in REM sleep (shown by the thick blue line at the top of each cycle).

depleted during sleep deprivation. Scientists think that the chemical reaction to restore glycogen, the brain's primary food, occurs during REM sleep. Sleep also may reinforce learning. The specific brain regions involved in learning a new task show increased patterns of activity during sleep the night after training. Also, sleep deprivation the night after learning a new task reduces performance of the same task the next day. Emotions become volatile if sleep is chronically disrupted, and thought processes are disturbed. In fact, prolonged sleep deprivation in humans can lead to temporary psychosis and hallucinations.

HOW THE BRAIN CONTROLS SLEEP

Scientists still do not know exactly what sleep is and what is happening in the brain when we sleep. Most of us think of

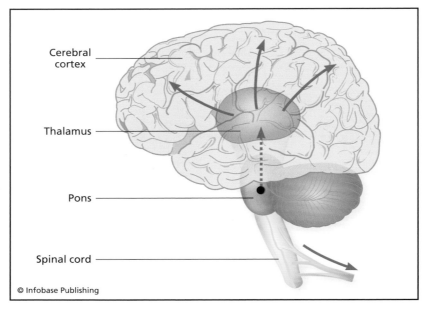

Cerebral
cortex

Thalamus

Pons

Spinal cord

© Infobase Publishing

Figure 8.2 Schematic showing the structures of the brain that are activated during the deepest stages of sleep. The pons, which is located in the brain stem, sends signals to the thalamus, which in turn activates many other areas of the brain. Conversely, signals sent via the spinal cord suppress muscular activity so that the body remains relaxed.

sleep as a restful time, but during some phases of sleep our brains are extremely active. During such sleep phases, a region deep in the brain, called the **pons,** sends excitatory activity to higher level structures in the brain that in turn activate other brain areas (Figure 8.2). Ultimately, many of the brain regions that process thoughts, memories, and emotion are involved. At the same time, the brain shuts down the spinal cord connections to muscles so that our bodies are reasonably relaxed and loose. Our brains cycle in and out of these active stages of sleep throughout the night.

A region in the hypothalamus of the brain called the **suprachiasmatic nucleus,** acts as a sort of natural pacemaker for the brain and body. It controls our **circadian rhythms**, which are roughly 24-hour cycles of primitive physiological processes, including waking and sleeping, temperature regulation, blood pressure, and even hormone production. The suprachiasmatic nucleus signals a gland in the middle of the brain called the **pineal gland** to secrete **melatonin**—a hormone that makes us feel sleepy. Melatonin is secreted at night so we can go to sleep, and production is stopped in the morning, allowing us to wake up bright-eyed and bushy-tailed.

The suprachiasmatic nucleus receives information from the eyes about the daily light and dark patterns (daytime and night-time). The brain uses this information to help set our sleep/wake cycles. Darkness helps trigger the release of melatonin and light suppresses melatonin release.

In the era before electrically generated light, we quite literally went to bed and got up "with the Sun" because our brains told us to do so. However, with the advent of bright artificial light, our brains can get confused occasionally and sleep/wake cycles can be disrupted. That is why sleep specialists typically recommend sleeping in a dark room at night. Also, too little light during the daytime can disrupt the normal cycle of melatonin suppression. Some sleep specialists believe that exposure to bright artificial light at specific times during the day can be helpful for people with sleep disorders. Research has also shown that exposure to bright light can have an antidepressant effect, especially in individuals who suffer from seasonal affective disorder, a tendency to suffer from depression most severely during the winter months, when there is less daylight.

Even though our brains use information about light and dark cycles to help synchronize sleep patterns, the cyclical nature of sleep and wakefulness can go on even in total darkness. The brain has an internal clock that will make us feel sleepy and then alert on a repeating cycle even in the absence of external cues such as the sun's rise and fall. The brain circuits that control circadian rhythms are extremely primitive and found in virtually all animal species. Thus, it had long been assumed that the mechanism that dictates when and how long we sleep is common to all humans and probably shows little natural variation across age except in the very young (who have high sleep requirements that may reflect rapid growth) and in the elderly (who for a number of reasons experience disrupted sleep cycles). Until only a few years ago, scientists had never thought to look at the factors that regulate sleep in adolescents to see if their chronic sleeplessness might be related to brain function.

DISRUPTED SLEEP PATTERNS IN ADOLESCENTS

To better understand the sleep habits of teenagers, the National Sleep Foundation conducted a survey in March of 2006. During telephone interviews with adolescents in grades 6–12 (ages 11–17 years) and their parents, information was gathered about the teens' sleep patterns. They found that average nightly amounts of sleep decline sharply as adolescents get older. For example, sixth graders reported sleeping an average of 8.4 hours on school nights. In contrast, twelfth graders admitted to getting only 6.9 hours of sleep on school nights. Yet experts at the National Institutes of Health have recommended that all school-aged children, including teens, need at least 9 hours of sleep daily.

The decrease in the average amount of sleep obtained by a teen probably takes place slowly over time but may reach problematic levels as early as the beginning of high school. The trend is caused by increasingly later bedtimes. Wake-up times tended to be consistent across all ages, at least on school days, because the start of the school day dictates the morning schedule.

Surprisingly, teens are well aware that they are not getting enough sleep. More than one fourth of the high school students admitted falling asleep in school, and nearly as many said they fall asleep while doing homework. Almost one fifth of all high school students report oversleeping on school days and occasionally either arriving late or missing school altogether.

Attempts to "catch up" on sleep lost during the school week are ineffective at best and may even degrade the amount and quality of subsequent nighttime sleep. More than 30% of teens reported that they take naps regularly. Parents might imagine that this is wonderful news, certainly a far cry from the nearly daily duels over naptime typical of preschool kids. However, scientists say that naps cannot be relied on as a replacement for a good night's sleep. In fact, sleep experts say that naps of longer than about 45 minutes can disrupt subsequent nighttime sleep. The surveyed teens reported that their naps last an average of 1.2 hours.

Sleeping in on weekends is another method teens use to catch up on lost sleep. Yet scientists believe that these irregular intervals of excessive sleep can further disrupt the biological clock. The brain can quickly adapt to shifts in sleep/wake cycles—just as it adjusts to travel across time zones. So when it gets confusing signals, such as the onset of wakefulness (and all the stimuli that accompany daytime activities) at noon rather than 7:00 A.M., it attempts to adjust by setting the subsequent nights' sleep cycle just that much later.

The consequences of sleep deprivation can affect nearly every part of a teen's life. In a study conducted by sleep expert Mary Carskadon and her research team at Brown University, the sleep habits of high school students were correlated with academic performance. Out of more than 3,000 high school students who were polled, those who reported making C's, D's, and F's admitted going to bed an average of 40 minutes later than students who reported making mostly A's and B's. It would be wrong to assume that these findings indicate that the poor academic performers are simply lazy. Instead, the data suggest that sleep deprivation has a significant detrimental impact on a teen's ability to learn. Other symptoms that have been attributed to insufficient sleep include irritability, depression, and daytime sleepiness.

SLEEP CYCLES SHIFT IN ADOLESCENT BRAIN

So now that it has been established that most teens suffer sleep deprivation, what can be done to address the problem? Here's an idea: Concerned parents should insist that their children go to bed earlier. Problem solved? Hardly.

Teens are not staying up until the wee hours of the night just to be cantankerous. They are not faking the sleepiness that envelops them long after the morning alarm has sounded. They are simply responding to the biological dictates of their

Obesity and Sleep Deprivation

Research evidence suggests that one of the factors that may contribute to obesity is an insufficient number of hours devoted to sleep per night. Sleep deprivation appears to disrupt hormones that regulate appetite, so people who sleep the least are the most likely to gain weight and to become obese. Evidence from other studies suggests that disrupted sleep may affect a wide array of hormones and other molecules that contribute to diseases such as cancer, heart disease, and diabetes.

Source: Rob Stein, "Scientists Finding Out What Losing Sleep Does to a Body," Washington Post, October 9, 2005. Available online. URL: http://www.washingtonpost.com/wp-dyn/content/article/2005/10/08/AR2005100801405.html

brains. For reasons that are unknown, the circadian rhythms set by teen brains are shifted, causing adolescent brains to be alert later at night and to remain in its sleep mode until later in the morning.

It is difficult to study the brain mechanisms that control circadian rhythms, even in bugs—a favorite experimental subject for many scientists trying to understand biological clocks. In humans, such studies are simply not feasible. The cells that regulate sleep are virtually inaccessible for direct study, located at the very base of the brain and near cells that control functions such as breathing and other basic life functions. Even imaging studies are impractical because the MRI scanner is loud (thus not conducive to sleep). Also, the patient needs to be actively doing something with his/her brain during a functional MRI scan so that the region of interest is active. However, a good alternative method for understanding how our brains regulate sleep is to study the production of melatonin, whose secretion is under the direct control of the suprachiasmatic nucleus (Figure 8.3).

There is one major potential complication with measuring melatonin. External triggers can affect its secretion. For example, staying up late and being exposed to light (possibly even the dim light coming from a television) can shift the brain's circadian clock. To adjust to the shift, the brain signals the pineal gland to adjust its production of melatonin. So a shift in melatonin production can be externally dictated—a big concern in studies of sleep habits of teens since they are notorious for their late nights. Thus, even though it had been known for years that melatonin secretion is different in young children compared to adolescents, it was unclear whether the lifestyle of teens (later bedtimes and thus later exposure to light) was responsible for shifting the body's sleep cycle.

Dr. Carskadon and her research team devised a creative way to control for external influences on melatonin levels.

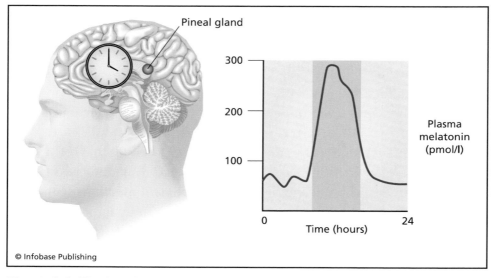

Figure 8.3 The location of the pineal gland is shown at left. The pineal gland secretes melatonin, which regulates our sleep/wake cycles. The plot at right shows how melatonin levels change over the course of a day. When melatonin is low, our brains are wakeful. At night, melatonin rises and triggers sleep (indicated by the vertical darker blue band). The rapid decrease of melatonin after sleep corresponds to morning and a return to wakefulness.

She recruited a wide range of teens who all agreed to maintain identical schedules, starting at home prior to the research experiment and continuing into the laboratory where the study was performed. This created the highest possible degree of certainty that the circadian rhythms of the teens were not being altered by external circumstances, such as watching a late-night movie. During the laboratory phase of the experiment, Dr. Carskadon and her colleagues collected melatonin samples from the saliva of the teens at specific times during the day and night. Their data were very compelling. In older adolescents, the melatonin levels rose later at night and fell off later in the morning compared to younger adolescents.

Since a rise in melatonin is what helps make us sleepy and ready for bed, the later onset of melatonin secretion discovered in older adolescents makes it extra difficult for them to even consider going to sleep. They may go to bed if they are told to, but the biochemistry of their brain might prohibit them from going to sleep. Conversely, if melatonin levels are still high in the morning when the alarm goes off, their brain's biochemistry screams that it is still nighttime. In fact, the brain is not fully awake and ready for business until melatonin levels drop to daytime lows. Yet Dr. Carskadon's team found that the melatonin offset time in older adolescents is not until around 9:30 A.M., well into the school day for most high school students.

The work of Dr. Carskadon and her team also offers an explanation for why "catch up" sleep is not the answer for sleep-deprived teens. Sleep appears to be affected by at least two different processes: one that regulates how much sleep we get and another that controls when in our circadian cycle we sleep. Apparently, our bodies not only need the right amount of sleep, but also we need sleep during the appropriate circadian phase. Naps fall during the wrong portion of the circadian cycle and probably do little to refresh the brain and body.

Narcolepsy

People who suffer from narcolepsy get overwhelming urges to sleep that can come on at any time and anywhere—even in the middle of a conversation or while driving a car. People with narcolepsy might fall asleep for just a few seconds or for several minutes. Only rarely do individuals remain asleep for stretches of an hour or longer. Narcolepsy occurs when the brain is unable to regulate sleep/wake cycles normally; however, its specific cause is unknown. People with narcolepsy also have difficulty sleeping through the night and the involuntary sleep episodes during the day may be the brain's way to catch up.

Finally, although biology is largely to blame for the shifts in sleep cycles during adolescent development, the lifestyle of teens can exacerbate the situation. Based on yet another study by the Carskadon team, it appears that older teens have different sensitivities to external influences than do their younger counterparts. For example, morning light is highly stimulating to young adolescents yet nighttime light does not have much impact on their sleep. Thus, they are chipper and ready for action nearly as soon as the sun comes up, but sleep soundly through the night even if parents peek in bringing a little hallway light in with them. Also, older adolescents appear to be less responsive to morning light but more susceptible to a light stimulus at night. Thus, a bright sunny morning is heralded with groans whereas a late-night movie actually can wake the brain up. Sleep-deprived teens need to help their brains know when it is time to go to sleep by turning off external stimuli such as televisions and computers that can confuse their sleep cycles.

■ **Learn more about the contents of this chapter**   Search the Internet for *rapid eye movement*, *sleep deprivation*, and *sleep and learning*.

9 | Putting It All Together

So what is the take-home message from the new research findings about the teen brain? It all depends on the perspective of the individual. At one extreme is the outlook that inspired a book titled, *Yes, Your Teen Is Crazy!* [6] In the same vein, an author of a magazine article wrote that the activity in the brain of teenagers is so intense, according to scientists, that it causes teens to be "emotionally and socially inept."[7] This probably is a minority opinion. In fact, for scientists, the prospect of exploring the teen brain through research is enthralling. Indeed, because the MRI and other imaging techniques are not harmful to the subject and have virtually no detrimental side effects, nearly every facet of the teenager brain likely will be explored in the near future.

From the perspective of parents, the evidence that the teen brain is still a work in progress may come as a source of comfort. It is disconcerting to a parent (most of whom have no formal training in child rearing before their kids are born) when they find themselves unable to understand or even relate to the stranger who occasionally takes over their child's body. This research may assure parents that the changes that accompany the teenage years are normal, even important.

For teens, perhaps having an understanding of the developmental changes that are taking place in the brain during the transition through adolescence will be encouraging. At the very least, it may be helpful to know that there is a scientific explanation for why teens do what they do. Their brains are not working like scientists had long thought—as a fully mature organ that simply needed life experience to help guide choices. Instead, we now know that brain function is still developing throughout much of the adolescent period.

Let's review some of what we have learned about the teen brain. First and perhaps most important, the surge in brain growth and refinement that takes place during adolescence provides a window of opportunity to maximize brain function. Best of all, scientists recommend that to build brain power all one has to do is to use one's brain in as many ways as possible including thinking, feeling, seeing, and doing. (So concentrating exclusively on math or music or soccer is not advisable!)

Keep in mind that a growing brain also is a vulnerable brain. Research suggests that the use of substances such as alcohol, marijuana, and other addictive drugs, particularly during the teenage years, may have a permanent, negative impact on brain function (Figure 9.1). This cannot be stressed enough. In fact, too much of anything will have undesirable consequences— even an overemphasis on academics at the expense of physical, social, and emotional development.

New research about the teen brain also explains why teens tend to seek out risky and sometimes even dangerous behaviors. Taking a risk—and overcoming it—activates the brain's reward circuits. However, the reward circuits in the adolescent brain function differently compared to those of adults. Some scientists speculate that teens' reward circuits need more activation than those of adults to experience a sense of pleasure from the reward.

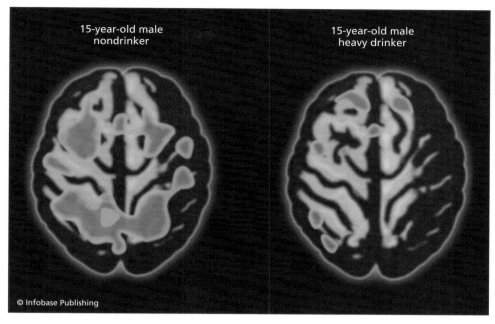

Figure 9.1 These brain images show a 15-year-old with an alcohol addiction (right) and 15-year-old non-drinker (left). The heavy drinker's brain shows considerably less brain activity (less pink and red coloration) when asked to perform a task.

To compound matters, teens may not even view some behaviors as risky. The prefrontal cortex, the area that is important for assimilating information, evaluating risk, and making decisions, is one of the last areas of the brain to develop. In fact, the prefrontal cortex may not be fully mature until the age or 20 or so. Thus, teens may quite literally think differently than adults.

Adults tend to be more deterred than teens are by the probability of risk. Also, adults are more motivated than teens by the chance of a reward—even a small reward and even if it takes a long time to achieve. Finally, adults tend to assume that everyone makes decisions using the same criteria as them, and they cannot comprehend that teens may choose a path that is, in adults' eyes, inconceivable. As a result, battles between parents and their teens over the choices that teens make may be unavoidable.

A note of caution is needed here for that small proportion of teens who tend to seek even higher levels of risk than the average adolescent. Most teens traverse their teenage years without suffering permanent long-term harm; however, young people are not invincible. In the absence of a mature prefrontal cortex, teens may not even comprehend that the consequences of some behaviors far outweigh the temporary rush provided by the brain's reward circuits. So it is important for teens to be sensitive to even the quietest voice in the deepest recesses of their brain. It may be the whispering of the slowly developing prefrontal cortex that has a reputation for giving good advice.

The evidence that diverse regions of the brain are influenced by the puberty hormones also helps shed light on adolescent behavior. Extreme emotional fluxes, glitches in recall, and inattention to tasks may reflect the impact of puberty hormones on brain structures sensitive to testosterone and/or estrogen. Although this evidence may not garner any extra consideration for teens by parents or teachers, it may at least comfort teens to know that what they are experiencing is a normal aspect of adolescent brain function.

Finally, now teens have proof that they are not sleeping the day away simply because they are lazy. Instead, their brain's internal clock is shifted. Thus, in teens, sleepiness and wakefulness occurs later than it does for adults.

In summary, puberty may be a trying time for many teens, but with support from friends and family—and their maturing brain—most are able to successfully navigate the emotional ups and downs and social changes that occur. In fact, today's teens are a fairly impressive lot. They serve in leadership positions in community government, in social justice programs, and in youth organizations. Perhaps J.K. Rowling, author of the Harry Potter books, summarizes it best: "Age is foolish and forgetful when it underestimates youth."[8]

Notes

1. Ryan, S.A., S.G. Millstein, and C.E. Irwin. "Puberty Questions Asked by Early Adolescents: What Do They Want to Know?" *Journal of Adolescent Health* 19 (1996),148–150.

2. Walsh, David. *Why Do They Act That Way? A Survival Guide to the Adolescent Brain for You and Your Teen* (New York, NY: Free Press, 2004), 1.

3. Wade, C. and C. Tavris. *Psychology* (New York, NY: Harper & Row Publishers, 1990), 504–505.

4. Goodall, Jane. *The Chimpanzees of Gombe* (Cambridge, Mass.: Harvard University Press, 1986), 166.

5. Macmillan, M. "Phineas Gage's Story." Deakin University. 2006. Available online at http://www.deakin.edu.au/hbs/psychology/gagepage/Pgstory.php.

6. Bradley, M.J. *Yes, Your Teen Is Crazy!: Loving Your Kid Without Losing Your Mind* (Gig Harbor, Wash.: Harbor Press, 2003).

7. Graham-Rowe, D. "Teen Angst Rooted in Busy Brain." *New Scientist.* 2002. Available online at http://www.newscientist.com/article.ns?id=dn2925.

8. Rowling, J.K. *Harry Potter and the Half-Blood Prince* (New York, NY: Scholastic Inc., 2005), 192.

Glossary

Action potential A wave of electrical activity that travels along the axon away from a cell body producing a release of neurotransmitter at the synapse.

Amygdala A region located deep in the temporal lobe of the brain that is involved in processing information that has emotional content.

Androgen receptor An intracellular receptor that binds testosterone and related hormones.

Axon The long slender extension from the nerve cell body that conducts the nerve impulse, or action potential, away from the cell body. Bundles of axons make up nerves.

Basal ganglia A complex of nerve cell clusters, called nuclei, located deep in the cerebral hemispheres that are involved with motor control, movement, and learning.

Cerebellum A large structure at the base of the brain that is involved in integration of sensory and perceptual information to fine-tune motor movements. The cerebellum also plays a role in higher thought processes, including attention. The word cerebellum is Latin for "little brain."

Cerebral cortex The outer layer of tissue that covers the surface of the brain.

Cerebral hemisphere One of the two symmetric halves that form the outermost shell of the brain.

Circadian rhythm An approximately 24-hour activity cycle of a wide range of biological processes, including sleep, thermal regulation, and hormonal secretion.

Cognitive Having to do with information processing, decision making, and intelligence.

Corpus callosum A large bundle of axons that connects the left and right cerebral hemispheres.

Critical period A time during development when there is a heightened sensitivity to external influences such as environmental stimuli and enrichment.

Dendritic field A richly branched field of processes, called dendrites that extend from the body of a nerve cell. Dendrites receive nerve impulses from other cells and conduct electrical signals toward the cell body.

Dopamine A neurotransmitter made by certain cells in the brain. Neurons that manufacture and secrete dopamine are involved in a wide array of brain functions, including motivation, emotion and movement.

Electroencephalograph A machine that measures the electrical activity in the brain.

Electrophysiological Pertaining to the electrical properties of biological structures. In the brain, electrophysiology involves measurements of the electrical events that contribute to the production of an action potential.

Estradiol One of several naturally occurring forms of estrogen, the female sex hormone.

Estrogen A hormone produced by a number of structures in the body that are responsible for the expression of secondary sex characteristics in females. Most estrogen is produced by the ovaries in females.

Estrogen receptor An intracellular protein that becomes activated in the presence of estrogen.

Follicle-stimulating hormone A hormone secreted by the anterior pituitary gland that stimulates the growth of follicles in the ovary and induces the formation of sperm in the testis.

Frontal lobe The most anterior region of the cerebral cortex, lying just behind the forehead.

Glia Non-neuronal cells that have a number of supporting roles in the brain, including the formation of myelin and recycling neurotransmitters after they are released from a neuron.

Gonadotropin-releasing hormone A hormone produced by cells in the hypothalamus beginning at puberty. Its presence triggers cells in the anterior pituitary gland to secrete luteinizing hormone and follicle-stimulating hormone.

Gray matter A nonspecific term that refers to regions of the brain and spinal cord that consist primarily of neuron cell bodies, glia, and their processes. The gray matter has a grayish color particularly in contrast to the white matter, which gets its whitish cast from myelinated axons. The outermost covering of the cerebral cortex consists of gray matter.

Hippocampus A region of the brain located in the temporal lobes that plays a critical role in memory formation and learning.

Hormone A chemical substance produced by glands and released into the bloodstream that can alter and control the function of specific target tissues.

Hypothalamus A structure located at the base of the brain that regulates critical bodily functions, including sleep cycles, body temperature, food and fluid intake, and blood pressure.

Limbic system An interconnected group of structures that plays a major role in the perception and expression of emotion and with the emotional aspects of memory.

Long-term potentiation (LTP) A long-lasting strengthening of the synaptic connections between two neurons.

Luteinizing hormone A hormone secreted by the pituitary gland that stimulates ovulation in females and initiates testosterone release in males.

Magnetic resonance imaging (MRI) A noninvasive diagnostic tool that uses a powerful magnetic field to excite atoms. The signals that are acquired when the atomic fields relax are used to generate computerized images of internal structures. The technique is best suited for imaging soft tissues.

Melatonin A hormone produced by the pineal gland that is involved in the regulation of the circadian cycle.

Meninges A three-layered membranous covering of the brain and spinal cord. The three layers include the dura mater, arachnoid, and the pia mater. Together they provide protection and nourishment to the central nervous system.

Menstruation The cyclical sloughing of the uterine lining, called the endometrium, that occurs in females of reproductive age.

Myelin A white, fatty material that surrounds many medium- and large-sized axons in the nervous system. Myelin provides protection for axons and greatly increases the speed of transmission of action potentials.

Neuron A cell found in the brain and spinal cord that is specialized to generate and transmit electrical impulses. A neuron consists of a cell body, dendrites, and one axon.

Neurotransmitter A chemical substance that is released at the synapse of a nerve cell. If the chemical encounters receptive sites on other nearby nerve cells, it will bind and initiate an electrical response in the target cell.

Nucleus accumbens A group of neurons involved in signaling the potential for obtaining reward, such as food or other pleasurable substances. It is thought to play an important role in addiction.

Olfaction The sense of smell.

Pineal gland A gland located near the center of the brain that secretes melatonin.

Pituitary gland A gland located at the base of the brain that secretes numerous hormones in response to hypothalamic activation. The hormones released by the pituitary gland regulate a wide array of biologic activities including growth, metabolism, blood pressure, thyroid gland function, and a range of reproductive functions.

Plasticity The capacity of a cell or one of its processes, a synapse or even molecules in the brain to change its physical or physiological characteristics.

Pons A structure located in the brain that is involved in a number of functions, including the transmission of sensory information, control of breathing, and sleep.

Prefrontal cortex The most anterior part of the frontal lobes, consisting of several different cortical areas that each has distinctive functions. In general, the region is responsible for planning, decision making, and personality.

Progesterone A hormone secreted by specific cells in the ovary that helps prepare for and maintain pregnancy. Progesterone also plays a role in the development of the mammary glands.

Sexually dimorphic nucleus of the preoptic area (SDN-POA) A group of cells located in the hypothalamus that shows substantial differences in size depending on gender, tending to be much larger in males than in females. It is believed to play a role in orchestrating some sexual behaviors.

Suprachiasmatic nucleus An area in the hypothalamus that contains neurons believed to be responsible for circadian rhythms. The suprachiasmatic nucleus receives neural inputs directly from the retina, so light and dark cycles can strongly influence the activity of its neurons.

Synapse The site at which one neuron connects to another neuron or to a muscle cell, or a secretory cell in a gland. The majority of synapses in the brain are chemical synapses, where a chemical (neurotransmitter) is released into a small space between two neurons. The impact on the target neuron depends on the properties of the receptor.

Synaptic activity The excitation or inhibition of electrical activity within one or more neurons.

Temporal lobe The portion of the cerebral hemisphere that is located on the side of the head, just above the ears.

Testosterone A hormone produced primarily by the testes that is responsible for male secondary sex characteristics.

Ventral tegmental area (VTA) A group of neurons located near the middle of the brain that is considered part of the reward circuit.

Ventricle A chamber in the brain through which cerebrospinal fluid circulates. The four ventricles in the brain are connected so that the fluid can circulate freely.

White matter A nonspecific term that refers to regions of the brain and spinal cord where myelinated axons are concentrated. Myelin is stark white so that bundles of myelinated axons are readily apparent in brain specimens. Few neurons are located in the white matter.

Working memory One type of memory that is used for temporarily storing information that might be needed for a subsequent task for decision making.

Bibliography

Baird, A.A. and J.A. Fugelsang. "The Emergence of Consequential Thought: Evidence from Neuroscience." *Philosophical Transaction of the Royal Society of London, Series B* 359 (2004): 1797–1804.

Bjork, J.M., B. Knutson, G.W. Fong, D.M. Caggiano, S.M. Bennett, and D.W. Hommer. "Incentive-elicited Brain Activation in Adolescents: Similarities and Differences from Young Adults." *Journal of Neuroscience* 24 (2004): 1793–1802.

Bruer, J.T. and W. Greenough. "The Subtle Science of How Experience Affects the Brain." In Bailey, D.B., J.T. Bruer, F.J. Symons and J.W. Lichtman. *Critical Thinking About Critical Periods.* Baltimore, Md.: Brookes Publishing (2001): 209–232.

Buonomano, D.V. and M.M. Merzenich. "Cortical Plasticity: From Synapses to Maps." *Annual Review of Neuroscience* 21 (1998): 149–186.

Carskadon, M.A., C. Acebo, G.S. Richardson, and B.A. Tate. "An Approach to Studying Circadian Rhythms of Adolescent Humans." *Journal of Biological Rhythms* 12 (1997): 278–289.

Chudler, E.H. "Brain Development." *Neuroscience for Kids.* 2006. Available online at http://faculty.washington.edu/chudler/dev.html.

Daw, N.D., J.P. O'Doherty, P. Dayan, B. Seymour, and R.J. Dolan. "Cortical Substrates for Exploratory Decisions in Humans." *Nature* 441 (2006): 876–879.

Galvan, A., T.A. Hare, C.E. Parra, J. Penn, H. Voss, G. Glover, and B.J. Casey. "Earlier Development of the Accumbens Relative to Orbitofrontal Cortex Might Underlie Risk-taking Behavior in Adolescents." *Journal of Neuroscience* 26 (2006): 6885–6892.

Giedd, J.N., J. Blumenthal, N.O. Jeffries, F.X. Castellanos, H. Liu, A. Zijdenbos, T. Paus, A.C. Evans, and J.L. Rapoport. "Brain Development During Childhood and Adolescence: A Longitudinal MRI Study." *Nature Neuroscience* 2 (1999): 861–863.

Gogtay, N., J.N. Giedd, L. Lusk, K.M. Hayashi, D. Greenstein, A. C. Vaituzis, T.F. Nugent III, D.H. Herman, L.S. Clasen, A.W. Toga, J.L. Rapoport, and P.M. Thompson. "Dynamic Mapping of Human

Cortical Development During Childhood Through Early Adulthood." *Proceedings of National Academy Science* 101 (2004): 8174–8179.

Goodall, Jane. *The Chimpanzees of Gombe*. Cambridge, Mass.: Harvard University Press, 1986.

Kaplowitz P.B., E.J. Slora, R.C. Wasserman, S.E. Pedlow, and M.E. Herman-Giddens. "Earlier Onset of Puberty in Girls: Relation to Increased Body Mass Index and Race." *Pediatrics* 108 (2001): 347–353.

Knoch, D., L.R.R. Gianotti, A. Pascual-Leone, V. Treyer, M. Regard, M. Hohmann, and P. Brugger. "Disruption of Right Prefrontal Cortex by Low-frequency Repetitive Transcranial Magnetic Stimulation Induces Risk-taking Behavior." *Journal of Neuroscience* 26 (2006): 6469–6472.

Llewellyn, D.J. "Risktaking." Risktaking.co.uk. 2003. Available online at http://www.risktaking.co.uk/index.htm.

Macmillan, M. "Phineas Gage's Story." Deakin University. 2006. Available online at http://www.deakin.edu.au/hbs/psychology/gagepage/Pgstory.php.

Malta, J.G. "Puberty 101." 2001. Available online at http://www.puberty101.com.

Manber, R., Bootzin, R.R., Acebo, C., and Carskadon, M.A. "The Effects of Regularizing Sleep-wake Schedules on Daytime Sleepiness." *Sleep* 19 (1996): 432–441.

Matthews, S.C., A.N. Simmons, S.D. Lane, and M.P. Paulus. "Selective Activation of the Nucleus Accumbens During Risk-taking Decision Making." *NeuroReport* 15 (2004): 2123–2127.

Menon, V., J.M. Boyett-Anderson, and A.L. Reiss. "Maturation of Medial Temporal Lobe Response and Connectivity During Memory Encoding." *Cognitive Brain Research* 25 (2005): 379–385.

Mohammed, A.H., S.W. Zhu, S. Darmopil, J. Hjerling-Leffler, P. Ernfors, B.K. Winblad, M.C. Diamond, P.S. Eriksson, and N. Bogdanovic. "Environmental Enrichment and the Brain." *Progress in Brain Research* 138 (2002): 109–133.

Monk, C.S., E.B. McClure, E.E. Nelson, E. Zarahn, R.M. Bilder, E. Leibenluft, D.S. Charney, M. Ernst, and D.S. Pine. "Adolescent Immaturity in Attention-related Brain Engagement to Emotional Facial Expressions." *NeuroImage* 20 (2003): 420–428.

Paus, T. "Mapping Brain Maturation and Cognitive Development During Adolescence." *Trends in Cognitive Sciences* 9 (2005): 60–68.

Ryan, S.A., S.G. Millstein, and C.E. Irwin Jr. "Puberty Questions Asked by Early Adolescents: What Do They Want to Know?" *Journal of Adolescent Health* 19 (1996): 145–152.

Saper, C.B. "Hypothalamus." In Paxinos, G., *The Human Nervous System*. San Diego, Calif.: Academic Press (1990): 389–414.

Manhart, K. "Lust for Danger." *Scientific American Mind*. 2005. Available online at http://www.sciammind.com/print_version. cfm?articleID=000ABC37-DD4E-1329-9CE283414B7F0000.

Sowell, E.R., P.M. Thompson, K.D. Tessner, and A.W. Toga. "Mapping Continued Brain Growth and Gray Matter Density Reduction in Dorsal Frontal Cortex: Inverse Relationships During Postadolescent Brain Maturation." *Journal of Neuroscience* 21 (2001): 8819–8829.

Spatz, H. "Hebb's Concept of Synaptic Plasticity of Neuronal Cell Assemblies." *Behavioural Brain Research* 78 (1996): 3–7.

Squire, L.R., J.L. Roberts, N.C. Spitzer, M.J. Zigmond, S.K. McConnell, and F.E. Bloom. *Fundamental Neuroscience, Second Edition*. San Diego, Calif.: Academic Press, 2003.

Toga, A.W., P.M. Thompson, and E.R. Sowell. "Mapping Brain Maturation." *Trends in Neurosciences* 29 (2006): 148–159.

Wade, C. and C. Tavris. *Psychology*. New York, NY: Harper & Row Publishers, 1990.

Walsh, David. *Why Do They Act That Way? A Survival Guide to the Adolescent Brain for You and Your Teen*, New York, NY: Free Press, 2004.

Wu, T., P. Mendola, and G.M. Buck. "Ethnic Differences in the Presence of Secondary Sex Characteristics and Menarche Among U.S. Girls:

The Third National Health and Nutrition Examination Survey, 1988–1994." *Pediatrics* 110 (2002): 752–757.

Yuste, R. and T. Bonhoeffer. "Morphological Changes in Dendritic Spines Associated with Long-term Synaptic Plasticity." *Annual Review of Neuroscience* 24 (2001): 1071–1089.

Further Reading

Squire, L.R., J.L. Roberts, N.C. Spitzer, M.J. Zigmond, S.K. McConnell, and F.E. Bloom. *Fundamental Neuroscience,* Second Edition. San Diego, Calif.: Academic Press, 2003.

Strauch, B. *The Primal Teen.* New York: Anchor Books, 2003.

Walsh, David. *Why Do They Act That Way? A Survival Guide to the Adolescent Brain for You and Your Teen.* New York: Free Press, 2004.

Web Sites

Alcohol and the Adolescent Brain
http://www.duke.edu/~amwhite/Adolescence/index.html

Family and Child Development: Adolescent Growth and Development
http://www.ext.vt.edu/pubs/family/350-850/350-850.html

Neuroscience for Kids—Brain Development
http://faculty.washington.edu/chudler/dev.html

NIMH: Teenage Brain: A Work in Progress
http://www.nimh.nih.gov/Publicat/teenbrain.cfm

Puberty 101
http://www.puberty101.com

Society for Neuroscience: Brain Briefings
http://www.sfn.org/?pagename=brainBriefings_chrolongical

Society for Neuroscience: Brain Facts
http://www.sfn.org/index.cfm?pagename=brainFacts

Stages of Intellectual Development in Children and Teenagers
http://www.childdevelopmentinfo.com/development/piaget.shtml

Picture Credits

Index

About the Author

Sherre Florence Phillips received her Ph.D. in the Department of Anatomy at Vanderbilt University and later joined Vanderbilt University's faculty in the Department of Psychology. She spent more than 21 years doing neuroscience research, exploring mechanisms of plasticity in adult and developing brains. Dr. Phillips attributes much of her expertise on adolescents to her son and daughter, whose teen years served as an in-home laboratory for this book. Currently, Dr. Phillips owns a science consulting firm in Nashville, Tennessee.

About the Editor

Eric H. Chudler, Ph.D., is a research neuroscientist who has investigated the brain mechanisms of pain and nociception since 1978. Dr. Chudler received his Ph.D. from the Department of Psychology at the University of Washington in Seattle. He has worked at the National Institutes of Health and directed a laboratory in the neurosurgery department at Massachusetts General Hospital. Between 1991 and 2006, Dr. Chudler was a faculty member in the Department of Anesthesiology at the University of Washington. He is currently a research associate professor in the University of Washington Department of Bioengineering and director of education and outreach at University of Washington Engineered Biomaterials.